W9-CKC-661

Talking Cure

Talking Cure

AN ESSAY ON
THE CIVILIZING POWER
OF CONVERSATION

Paula Marantz Cohen

PRINCETON UNIVERSITY PRESS
PRINCETON & OXFORD

Published by Princeton University Press
41 William Street, Princeton, New Jersey 08540
99 Banbury Road, Oxford OX2 6JX

press.princeton.edu

ISBN 978-0-691-23850-0
ISBN (e-book) 978-0-691-23851-7

Library of Congress Control Number: 2022946324

British Library Cataloging-in-Publication Data is available

Editorial: Peter Dougherty and Alena Chekanov
Production Editorial: Karen Carter
Text Design: Karl Spurzem
Jacket/Cover Design: Lauren Smith
Production: Erin Suydam
Publicity: Kathryn Stevens and Maria Whelan
Copyeditor: Joseph Dahm

Jacket/Cover Credit: *In a coffee shop* © Giada Canu / Stocksy

This book has been composed in Arno with Swear

Printed on acid-free paper. ∞

Printed in Canada

10 9 8 7 6 5 4 3 2 1

For my sister, Rosetta

Contents

Preface

My mother used to tell me that as a baby I cried continuously when left alone in my crib but became smiley and happy whenever people were around. It seemed that, almost from birth, company uplifted and enlivened me, a trend that continues to this day. When I am alone or without interaction, I tend to fall into despondency that lifts as soon as I engage with someone else.

I find myself often plagued with insomnia, perhaps a return to the bereftness of infancy. One of the pastimes I indulge in when I can't fall asleep is to imagine a dinner party with people from history whom I admire and with whom I imagine I would enjoy conversing. Some individuals that crop up in this day-dream: Michel de Montaigne; Samuel Johnson; George Eliot; Frederick Douglass; Henry, William, and Alice James; Virginia Woolf and Vanessa Bell; Sigmund Freud; Sinclair Lewis; Mary Pickford and Douglas Fairbanks; Gregory Bateson; Jean-Paul Sartre and Simone de Beauvoir; James Baldwin; Lionel and Diana Trilling; Alfred Hitchcock; and Christopher Hitchens.

This is a largely white and fairly male-heavy group, reflecting my coming of age in the seventies in Western culture. I won't apologize for that since I did not choose when I was born. Moreover, these figures have been a source of inspiration and enlightenment to me and have led me beyond themselves to see the gaps and biases inherent in the traditions they represent.

I have taken pleasure in their work, and I believe they would be interesting, profound, or very clever in conversation (Hitchens is the only one whom I actually met, about a year before his death, and he was delightful!). In the case of the couples listed (Doug and Mary; Simone and Jean-Paul; the Trillings), I would be content to listen to them talk for insight into their known-to-be-fraught relationships. In the case of the siblings (Henry, William, and Alice; Virginia and Vanessa), to observe their probably fascinating but dysfunctional family dynamics.

I realize that some of these people could be disappointing in the flesh. There is often a great disparity between people's representation of themselves in controlled settings and their presence without a script. I was once deeply disappointed watching a television interview with that most deft of on-screen personas, Fred Astaire—he was excruciatingly ill at ease and shy. Even when people are supposed to be good conversationalists, the expectation that they be so can be inhibiting. I've known people reduced to doltishness after being told that they had a reputation for wit.

Conversation under the wrong circumstances can also devolve quickly and become boring—or nasty. Sartre wrote a play about this titled *No Exit* in which, as one of the characters put it, "hell is other people." But, then, the opposite can be true as well. When the setting is right and the companions sympatico, "heaven is other people." Which I imagine would be the case at my hypothetical dinner party.

Rest assured that I would not invite these figures all together. One of the mistakes people make (and I've made) when they throw dinner parties is that they have too many guests. A cocktail party is one thing; it is meant to feature insubstantial fare, both intellectual and culinary (chitchat and hors d'oeuvres—

and plentiful drink to provide an illusion of more ample engagement). But a dinner happens around a table and should involve sustained and substantive talk involving the group as a whole. One can't exceed ten for this kind of thing, and, even then, the possibility of true, communal intercourse is unlikely. Eight or, better, six is advisable. ("Six is about the right size" for dinner conversation, agreed W. H. Auden in his poetry collection, *About the House.*) The larger a dinner gets, the greater the risk of one or two blowhards dominating the event or of having the group splinter into nattering twosomes. It is the job of the host, like that of the teacher in a seminar, to prevent this from occurring. But when the numbers become too great, even the most skillful host can lose her grip.

In the case of the above list, it is fun for me to imagine how they might be grouped for the most effective conversation. Alice James and Frederick Douglass—yes! Simone de Beauvoir and Alfred Hitchcock?—possibly. Sigmund Freud and Dr. Johnson?—no!—but throw in George Eliot, and it might work. It is interesting to think how people can combine, like ingredients in recipes, heightening or diluting each other, or producing some felicitous new combination.

The rendering of dinner-table talk is a genre of sorts going back to Plato's *Symposium.* Lucian's *Dialogues of the Courtesans* and *Dialogues of the Dead* presumably took their cue from Plato but were satirical rather than philosophical. *Table Talk* miscellanies were popular in the nineteenth century, with Samuel Taylor Coleridge's contribution being the most noteworthy. The volume covered such topics as "Reason and Understanding," "Jews," "Greek and Latin Pentameter," "Characterlessness of Women," and "Times of Charles I." One can practically hear Coleridge's exhaustively erudite chatter as one peruses this book. In the 1920s, *Vanity Fair* magazine created a series of "Impossible Interviews," which featured imagined conversations between the likes of Will Rogers and Noel Coward, John D. Rockefeller Sr. and Joseph Stalin, and Greta Garbo and Calvin Coolidge. Alexander Woollcott, a member of the Algonquin Circle, turned this idea into a literal exercise, bringing unlikely people together in what he dubbed "Strange Bedfellows" (one incongruous pair that got along surprisingly well was Harpo Marx and George Bernard Shaw!). More recently, Craig Brown, the English satirist, described a daisy chain of eccentric real-life encounters in *Hello Goodbye Hello: A Circle of 101 Remarkable Meetings*. In some cases—Mark Twain and Helen Keller—the rapport is immediate; in others—Groucho Marx and T. S. Eliot—the personalities rub each other the wrong way just as quickly.

My own experience suggests that, whatever one may think in advance, one never can tell how people will get along. Some of my acquaintances who seem bound to like each other, don't; and some who seem incompatible, do. I know a number of people whom I should not logically like conversing with whom I nonetheless find invigorating, and several who seem perfect on paper whom I avoid like the plague. Human personality is an odd and delicate mechanism, and our predilections and aversions can be tipped in one direction or the other by elements as fine as a butterfly's wing.

When I was approached to write a book about conversation, I responded enthusiastically. If there's one thing I like to do more than anything else, it's talk. Everyone needs conversation, but some people need more of it than others. I am someone who needs more, and to write about the topic seems to me almost as good as engaging in it. In this, I diverge radically from the classical philosopher Epictetus, who, in his collection of *Golden Sayings*, cautioned,

> Let silence be your general rule; or say only what is necessary and in few words . . . , avoiding such common topics as gladiators, horse-races, athletes; and the perpetual talk about food and drink. . . . If you can, win over the conversation of your company to what it should be by your own. But if you should find yourself cut off without escape among strangers and aliens, be silent.

I would violate Epictetus's closing maxim on the spot. Instead of being silent, I would work diligently to find something to say. Strangers and aliens—especially aliens!—would pose a particular challenge. My kinship is with Montaigne, who spent an inordinate amount of time writing rather than conversing but who nonetheless observed, "The most fruitful and natural exercise of the mind, in my opinion, is conversation; I find the use of it more sweet than any other action of life."

George Bernard Shaw, a notorious windbag, has one of the characters in his play *Candida* observe, "If you want original conversation, you better go talk to yourself." Of course, this misses the point, and even Shaw acknowledges as much when another character rejoins, "But it's horribly lonely not to hear someone else talk sometimes." More than sometimes. The reason we converse is to forget our existential aloneness, to get out of our own heads, and replenish our sense of connectedness to others. When a conversation works, nothing is more joyful, more satisfying, and more affirmative of life. Now more than ever, if we are to preserve what is best in ourselves and our society, we need good conversation. In this book, I explore why that is and how we can try to make it happen.

Talking Cure

Introduction

I come from a family of talkers. The household in which I grew up was always noisy. My parents were loud and opinionated, and interrupted and quarreled boisterously with each other. I realize that such an environment could give rise, in opposition, to taciturn children who seek quiet above all else. But for me, the prevailing atmosphere felt comforting and safe. It made my childhood home a place I loved to be.

The bright, ongoing talk that pervaded my growing up was overseen by my mother, a woman of great charm and energy. She was the maestro of the dinner table, unfailingly entertaining and fun. We loved to listen to her tell stories about what happened to her at work. She was a high school French teacher, a position that afforded a wealth of anecdotes about her students' misbehavior, eccentric wardrobe choices, and mistakes in the conjugation of verbs. There were also the intrigues among her colleagues—how I loved being privy to my teachers' peccadillos and romantic misadventures, an experience that sowed a lifelong skepticism about authority. My mother had the gift of making even the smallest detail of her day vivid and amusing.

My father, by contrast, was a very different kind of talker. A scientist by training and vocation, he had a logical, detached sort of mind, and his subjects for discussion were ideas. He had theories about things: why people believed in God, the role of advertising in modern life, why women liked jewelry, and so on.

I recall how he would clear his throat as a prelude to launching into a new idea: "I've been thinking about why we eat foods like oysters and lobster, which aren't very appealing. There must be an evolutionary aspect to why we have learned to like these things." Being included in the development of an idea with my father was a deeply bonding experience. The *idea* of ideas became enormously appealing as a result. And though my father was not an emotional person—and indeed, because he was not—ideas became imbued with feeling in being associated with my relationship with him.

My talk with my parents was not entirely reciprocal. They led and I followed. But, then, they were my parents and not my peers. I expected them to know things I didn't and to control the direction of our talk.

The case was different with my sister. Siblings present us with unique challenges. Because we arrive in our families at different times, we are inevitably thrust into hierarchical relationships and must learn through acts but also, and perhaps more importantly, through words, how to share. For me, the transition from older sister to equal partner in conversation with my sister was particularly difficult, perhaps because she and I were so superficially similar in interests and talents (her talents in many ways superior to mine). For a long time, I clung to the status of older sister as the one element of superiority that I could continue to claim. I still sometimes feel myself trying to one-up or overexplain to my sister, but I have fought against this tendency; I have come to see the sibling relationship as a practice space for conversational relationships outside the family that requires equality and reciprocity to be authentic and satisfying.

My mother died over twenty-five years ago of a progressive neurological illness, and though we continued to communicate until almost the end, her ability to tell me stories and to perform for me diminished as she grew sicker. My father died last year after being slowly taken over by dementia. Over the previous two years, he more or less stopped talking. This was sadder for me than the diminishment of my mother before her death, which still allowed for our emotional connection, but it was also less difficult to handle. Since my relationship to my father was almost entirely intellectual, that loss of our ability to share ideas made him seem like another person, the mere shell of what he had been. And so, though his body, still relatively healthy until the end, recalled the past, it didn't actually denote the person. I realize that I marked my father's passing from the time he stopped being able to engage with me intellectually.

My conversation with my sister continues. It is a vital part of my life. Though not the same kind of conversation that we had as children and I think far more equal than it once was, it carries the imprint of that earlier time. We often talk about the past, about our differing views of our childhood and our parents, and about our aspirations for ourselves and our children. There is an undertow to sibling conversation—an antecedent life that moves beneath the words, that allows for shared hilarity at things that others don't find funny, and for understanding of the most minor and seemingly trivial inflections or facial expressions (siblings can get angry at each other for a fleeting smile or raised eyebrow that no one else would ever notice). My sister and I are attuned to each other this way, but also aware of how our past in the family can pull us down, which makes us extremely careful and conscientious with each other.

I have described my family of origin in some detail to offer one template for the relatively closed system in which we all begin our lives and gain the tools by which we proceed to communicate beyond it. If I learned how to talk in my family of origin, that original space was, for all its liveliness and interest, narrow in its scope and idiosyncratic in its lexicon. This is the paradox of growing up. Language is learned in the family; it is the means of both solidifying our place within it and allowing us to move beyond it, giving us the tools to widen our experience with people very different from ourselves.

Most of us are destined to outgrow our families of origin—thrown by necessity into the world by school and friendships that develop early and help us move away from that first, inbred space. But living in a larger world is difficult, and it is easier to embrace thinking and behavior that recapitulates in some way the safety of that initial family. Sects of various kinds (and I use the term "sect" loosely) are insidious in that they provide an illusion of freedom from our past while keeping us confined to ideas and values that never get a chance to be tested, elaborated, or changed. And they make those outside of our group seem strange and threatening.

Marriage—or long-term, intimate partnership—is a special case. I recall a friend telling me before I got married that my union with this other person would allow me to refresh the subjects and style of conversation to which I had become habituated. This was certainly true in the beginning. And indeed, it makes the early stages of intimacy difficult. When we live in proximity with someone else, we have to adjust ourselves to a discourse developed in another family of origin and that can be awkward and even unpleasant, a wrenching away from what we know and feel comfortable with. Ultimately, it is a process of synthesis—of our own lexicon with that of the other person—and I estimate that it took my husband and me half a dozen years or so to achieve this.

Eventually, however, if the relationship persists and deepens, one develops a new kind of predictable language, as second nature as the discourse we were bred to. In creating our own families, we can't help but close ourselves off again, to some degree, from the larger world, replacing one kind of circumscribed vocabulary with another. This can provide a sense of safety and well-being, useful, especially if children are involved, but also a barrier to free exchange with what lies beyond. For in becoming predictable and known, conversation within the family—whether the family of origin or the family we make—cuts us off from difference. To speak to the converted or the entirely familiar is not to truly converse. It is to have one's beliefs reinforced; it is self-soothing but not self-developing.

In past eras, daily life made it necessary for individuals to engage with others different from themselves. Families were larger and more extended rather than small and closed, and so people were often in contact with cousins and more distant relatives of the sort we see now only at Thanksgiving or know about through Ancestry.com. It's true that pronounced ethnic, religious, and class barriers kept various groups apart from each other in unjustly prescribed ways. Nonetheless, the serendipity of having to move around in literal space created unpredictable encounters. People were forced to engage with others in order to carry on the business of their lives.

That element of serendipity has now diminished. For all our espousal of difference and diversity, we have become a nation of factions and tribes, our thinking, in so many instances, hardened into repetitive patterns of agreement or opposition. The rise of social media, while it provides access to people in far-flung places, also supports a narrow sectarianism of ideas and feeds mockery and mean-spiritedness. The COVID-19 pandemic has exacerbated these tendencies of isolation and repetition. Many people nowadays engage only with those whose views and life experiences mirror their own.

But to recirculate the same ideas within a closed group is likely to poison our sense of those outside that group and make society a site of continual conflict and enmity. And perhaps

worse is the harm we do ourselves. If we simply mouth plati-
tudes of agreement, we must harbor the secrets of our individual
natures within our own breasts, and this can turn toxic to our
mental health. To share who we are, in our essential uniqueness,
is one of the most human and creative of acts. I believe that most
all of us need good conversation to lift our spirits, connect us to
others, and give us a more solid sense of ourselves.

Hope, as I see it, lies on the local and intimate level of conversations between friends, colleagues, and strangers over
lunch, dinner, and coffee; in the supermarket line or waiting for
the bus—finding some kind of common ground, even as we
disagree about politics, religion, and the meaning of life. The
inevitable fact of mortality looms over us all and can lead us to
put our differences in perspective: to make each other laugh
and to laugh at ourselves, to share an awareness of the incongru-
ity of things, and to question, together, the premises that we
hold dear but which may be wrong or incomplete. These subjects bind us to each other and inform our best conversations.

CHAPTER 1

Why Converse?

The title of this book, *Talking Cure*, derives from Sigmund Freud's pioneering approach to dealing with his patients. Freud began his work as a physician in Vienna in the late nineteenth century. During his early career, before having codified the new field of psychoanalysis, he noted that many patients presented with physical symptoms that had no apparent somatic cause. He eventually concluded that these symptoms—a chronic cough or a paralyzed limb, for example—were psychosomatic responses to traumatic events or taboo desires, often dating from childhood, that the patients were unable to face or comprehend. He found that if they could be encouraged to talk without inhibition—to free associate on what they were feeling—they would eventually, with the help of their therapist, find the source of the problem and the cure for their symptoms. Recognizing this, Freud made talk central to his therapeutic method.

Freud developed the initial idea of talk therapy in concert with his colleague Joseph Breuer whose patient, known in his annals as Anna O (her real name was Bertha Pappenheim), coined the phrase "talking cure." Freud later collaborated more closely with others, most famously Carl Jung, who, in a 1959 interview, two years before his death, referred to the "long and penetrating conversations" he had with Freud before their falling out (presumably at Freud's instigation) in 1913. Unfortunately, lots of talking can also give rise to lots of opportunities for giving offense, especially if the participants are opinionated, strong-willed, and engaged in laying the groundwork for a new field of study.

Despite these pitfalls, Freud seems to have enjoyed conversation with friends and colleagues throughout his life. This, I believe, was a function of his personality, which was expressive and gregarious (if also arrogant and self-protecting). It may also have been the legacy of his Jewish heritage that valued intellectual exchange. The ancient rabbis were devoted to ongoing discussion of the Torah and codified their commentary in the form of the Talmud and Midrash. It has been said that Freud's psychoanalytic writings were the extension of this Jewish tradition of rabbinical commentary into a secular context.

If the Torah represents a religious people's conversation with God, psychoanalysis, one could argue, represents their conversation with themselves, rendering God obsolete (or so Freud, who had no use for religion and ridiculed it directly in several of his works, could be said to argue).

Although many of Freud's theories regarding psychological processes have been superseded by chemical explanations of brain function, the "talking cure" has endured. Clinical psychologists still recommend talk therapy as treatment for both standard neurosis and more severe mental illness (though often in conjunction with medication). And though Freud's "talking cure" is not, by any stretch, a real conversation in the sense that I am proposing to discuss it in this book—the patient talks, the analyst listens and strategically intervenes—the phrase "talking cure" strikes me as a useful one with regard to my topic here.

The need for conversation is one that many people have not fully acknowledged, perhaps because they have not had occasion to do enough of it or to do it well. I am not suggesting that, in conversing, we serve as each other's therapists, but I do believe that good talk, when carried on with the right degree of openness, can not only be a great pleasure but also do us a great deal of good, both individually and collectively as members of society.

If much of Freud's work has been scientifically discredited, it has been enormously influential outside the realm of clinical psychology, especially in the areas of literary and philosophical theory. Freud wrote with seeming spontaneity and fluency as though he were engaging in conversation with the reader—stylistic attributes appreciated by literary scholars and critics. His use of abstract concepts, metaphors, and extended analogies for things that we cannot literally see or lay our hands on, remains deeply evocative to those concerned with the relationship of language to ideas and behavior. As a result, his theories still resonate with people interested in exploring how our interactions with others shape us over time and how talking about them can be a therapeutic activity.

For me, one particularly useful concept derived from Freud's talking cure is the idea of *transference*. In the course of therapy, Freud found that patients often felt that they had fallen in love with their therapists. Since he believed that all love relationships recapitulate what occurs within one's family of origin, he saw these patients' infatuation as a repetition of earlier, intense feelings for a parent that could now be analyzed and controlled—directed toward more productive and transparent ends.

I think this idea is relevant to our understanding of conversation as an important activity in connecting us with others. Putting aside the familial baggage that Freud saw as accompanying transference, a deep sense of affection seems to me to be always part of good conversation as we experience it as social beings. Surely, my readers can identify with that welling of positive feeling—that almost-falling-in-love-with someone with whom we engage on an authentic level. I have felt this not only for friends and even strangers with whom I've had a probing or even a fleeting conversation but also for whole classes of students where it can seem that the group has merged into one deeply lovable and loving body.

If love can be understood as important in conversation, so can desire, another element that derives from Freud's thought. Sexual desire has its consummation in the sex act—a temporary closure that accounts for why John Donne and other metaphysical poets use "death" to refer to sexual climax, giving them an evocative and amusing pun to work with. Conversation, by contrast, does not consummate; it merely stops by arbitrary necessity. You may have to end it in order to get across town for a meeting, pick up a child from school, or generally get on with the business of life. Such endings are *in medias res*, so to speak. I find it interesting that relationships can sometimes be over once the partners have consummated it in sex. But friendships are never over after a good conversation; they are sustained by it.

The relationship of conversation to desire may be better understood if we draw on the work of Jacques Lacan, the French psychoanalyst seen as the postmodern heir to Freudian theory. Lacan's neo-Freudian model, using material from the early twentieth-century linguist Ferdinand de Saussure, saw language as the primary structuring agent for desire of any kind. This was fundamental to his notion of the unconscious. Freud conceived of the unconscious as a cauldron of unfiltered, chaotic impulses, but Lacan famously redefined this domain with the dictum "the unconscious is structured like a language." In other words, we remain inside the lexicon of our society's language even in the way our impulses and drives manifest themselves.

Lacan's writing can be frustratingly cryptic, but I take from it certain fundamental ideas that strike me as relevant to our need to converse with each other. According to Lacan, we operate in the world out of a sense of incompleteness or "lack," experienced when, as infants, we undergo separation from the mother and enter the symbolic order of language under the rule of the father. This gender division (which Lacan meant to reflect normative ideas built into the culture) may be becoming obsolete, but the concept of desire as operating under the rule of language continues to ring true. We are continually drawn from one symbol or configuration of meaning to another.

This search on the part of our desiring self seems to me at the heart of good conversation. We seek to fill the lack in ourselves by engaging with someone who is Other—who comes from another position, another background, another set of experiences. Everyone, when taken in a certain light, is an Other by virtue, if nothing else, of having different DNA. To both recognize this difference and to be welcoming of it is the premise upon which good conversation is built.

Central to Lacan's thinking (and arguably to Freud's as well) is the idea that there is no "great Other"—no God or Godlike figure, no "transcendental signifier" (in the phrase of the deconstructionist philosopher Jacques Derrida)—only a chain of signifiers, a continual movement from one temporary meaning to another that can never settle into certainty or stasis. This, I would argue, is the source of the frustration that we can feel at never quite coming to the end of an idea, but also the joy of always finding new meaning and insight to be plumbed.

The contemporary psychoanalyst and philosopher Adam Phillips has addressed these ideas from a complementary perspective. He argues that change is inevitable in human life while also being disruptive and frightening. We must, by definition, change, but we fear change and do what we can to avoid it. This is why, according to Phillips, we are vulnerable to being *converted*—to an ideology, a movement, or a religion—where we can bypass uncertainty and feel we have managed to stop change. Phillips has written about the lengths to which some people go in seeking totalizing meaning or absolute closure. Freud's patients did this by converting their fears and traumas into symptoms and were able to break free only when they engaged in the free association of the talking cure.

Conversation has a similarly therapeutic effect for those of us who fear change, even if we are not, like Freud's patients, suffering crippling symptoms. Talk with others allows us to practice uncertainty and open-endedness in a safe environment. It exercises us in extemporaneity and experiment—it *de*converts us from our rigid and established forms of belief. There is no better antidote for certainty than ongoing conversation with a friend who disagrees with us on a range of matters.

I say this from my own experience. Forty years ago, when I began teaching at Drexel University, where I am still employed, I met a colleague, fifteen years older than I was and very different from me in background and perspective on life. Dave Jones came from Kansas, had served in the Marines in Viet Nam, and was a staunch political conservative. I grew up in New Jersey, a Jewish woman from a left-leaning family (going back to my grandfather, whose brother had been an active Bolshevik, purged by Stalin). Yet Dave and I were able to forge a strong, if sometimes volatile, friendship. We talked several times a week over lunch during the course of our thirty-five years as colleagues (one of the great advantages of the academic life is that it allows for this kind of desultory and regular talk, as I shall discuss further in chapter 9).

When Dave died several years ago, I realized that my worldview had been indelibly altered by my ongoing conversations with him. I just couldn't see things in the uninflected way that I might have done had we not conversed with energy and goodwill (at least most of the time) on subjects ranging from our views on abortion to our taste in movies. What sustained us in our disagreement was our mutual respect, indeed deep affection, for each other. It was a feeling that carried moral as well as emotional weight.

This is where Freud and his successors fall short. They are a great resource for exploring the dynamics of relationship, but their models for human interaction lack a moral context. This is understandable. Where individuals are in psychic pain, healing must take precedence over ethical issues.

But conversation is a social activity. Although it can have therapeutic value, it must involve respect for those with whom one engages to be genuine rather than feigned or performative. I have already mentioned how Freud's idea of transference brings love into the analytic picture. But Freud's notion of love is primarily sexual in nature (though capable of being productively *displaced*), derived from his concept of the libido as the primary drive in human life. By contrast, conversation, occurring entirely in the realm of the symbolic order of language, can be said to translate love into respect and affection. It recognizes the humanity of the Other within the context of society.

I connect this humanizing emotion that arises out of good conversation to the teachings of eighteenth-century moral philosopher Immanuel Kant. Kant is sometimes faulted for promoting a rigid sense of morality that fails to account for the vicissitudes of real-world interaction. And yet Kant's Categorical Imperative, when taken as a generalized litmus test for human relationships, seems to me to support what occurs in good conversation.

The second formulation of Kant's Categorical Imperative has been termed the "Humanity Formula" because it explicitly takes into account the human aspect of our engagement with the world: "never act in such a way that we treat humanity, whether in ourselves or in others, as a means only but always also as an end in itself." To translate: *don't treat other people like objects*. When we recognize the full humanity of others, we are true to ourselves and to them in a way that is not competitive, not exploitative, and not instrumental or utilitarian—or, at least, not *only* so. While a conversation can be useful to us—can gain us a job by showcasing our strengths, or provide us with emotional support in a time of need—it is only moral and truly satisfying when we see our fellow conversant as a complex human being, not as a means to an end.

This is why most conversations for the purpose of diplomacy and political debate are not real conversations—they are a means to the end of persuading a person or an audience to believe or do something. And yet it has been noted that some diplomats and statesmen have been able to forge a personal rapport with the individual with whom they are engaging that somehow transcends the utilitarian nature of their relationship. This is said to be the case for Winston Churchill and Franklin Roosevelt (with the help of cigars and whiskey—or champagne and cognac), of Ronald Reagan and Mikhail Gorbachev (and Reagan and Tip O'Neill across the aisle), and of Richard Nixon and Zhou Enlai. Admittedly, the personal rapport may well be part of a promotional campaign to create a climate of goodwill and support the end in view, but there is no denying that at times individuals *as* individuals emerge in conversation, even when it is tightly scripted or directed. Yet it has also been suggested that a friendship between world leaders can inhibit rather than support good foreign policy since it can cloud instrumental judgment (speculated to have been the case between George W. Bush and Vladimir Putin).

These musings lead me to another thinker who adds an element of social integration to the prescription laid out by Kant: the Russian philosopher and literary critic Mikhail Bakhtin. His model of engagement includes three components: I-for-myself, I-for-the-Other, and the-Other-for-me. Bakhtin saw this triad as fundamental in building community. "I-for-myself" is essentially inert, but "I-for-the-Other" leads to incorporating others into oneself, and "the-Other-for-me" into the incorporation of oneself into others. Bakhtin connects this interpenetration of self and others to a specific communal event—the historic form of celebration known as "carnival," where conventional behavior is turned on its head and barriers between people who would normally be unable to relate to each other are broken down.

Bakhtin's most intriguing work focuses on literature—and on the novel, in particular, as a genre that he sees as uniquely "dialogic": possessing that interplay of unencumbered perspectives associated with carnival. Novels, for Bakhtin, provide us with a means of experiencing the multiple voices of a creative and expressive humanity. As a teacher of literature, I can vouch for this: read great works and this will enhance your fund of empathy and insight. I am convinced that I decided to study literature so that I could read books, especially novels, unimpeded and immerse myself in their dialogic nature—but also so that I could talk about the ideas and feelings I derived from these books with my peers and eventually with my students. In the process, I could assimilate the nuance and contradiction that this literature dramatizes but also incites.

Literature, one could say, is an important resource for conversation because it is a kind of prosthetic expression of the self. Being exposed to characters in fiction who have been created empathetically by their authors can supply a road map for not only how to think more empathetically about others but how to feel connected to something that would otherwise fall outside our experience. A character like Anna Karenina, if seen entirely from the outside, would be hard to sympathize with, but after reading Tolstoy's novel, we do, if we have any degree of sensitivity, even if we still see her actions as profoundly wrongheaded, even sinful. Literary characters, when well drawn, are neither saints nor sinners, and this becomes a lesson about humanity (one, unfortunately, contradicted by bad literature that tends to operate in black-and-white terms). I will return to this idea in later chapters when I discuss the value of the college seminar and my experience reading Shakespeare on Zoom.

One might argue that authentic conversation is doomed when we exist inside ideological positions that limit us in predictable ways. While it is true that partisanship has become more pronounced in recent years (and seems at times to have usurped individual judgment), I don't think that this is an irreparable state of being. Conversation—probing and spirited—can break apart ossified patterns of thought and bring us to a more generous view of each other. I have experienced the exhilaration of having an insight that didn't fit with my preexisting ideas and of connecting with someone I might otherwise have written off. Most of us fear talking about important subjects with people we know disagree with us, much the way we fear talking to people about the untimely death of a loved one. And yet these conversations are often, secretly, what both parties crave.

I would be remiss in ending this grab bag of theorizing as it relates to conversation not to draw from anthropology and the dynamics of gift giving. The great anthropologist Marcel Mauss explained gift giving as an exchange outside of commodity culture—one in which the gift carries the imprint of the self and calls out for reciprocation. Gift giving, according to Mauss, is a "total social fact": it encapsulates the mutuality of giving, receiving, and reciprocating. The best conversations feel like such exchanges—gifts of insight, feeling, and opinion between or among individuals, noncommodifiable but precious in being reciprocal. If carried on over time, they become an ineffable part of ourselves.

Finally, I have not addressed the sheer pleasure of using words in original ways. If writing and speechifying can be equated with sculpture, where one models something through words in solitary space, conversation is more like certain kinds of sports, where the game proceeds within certain parameters but is unpredictable and reliant on one's ability to coordinate with another person or persons. Words in conversation can be arranged in infinite ways, but they wait on the response of a partner or partners, making this an improvisational experience partially defined by others and requiring extreme attentiveness to what they say. Also like sport, conversation requires some degree of practice to do well. The more one converses—and with a variety of people—the better one gets at it and the more pleasure it is likely to bring.

The analogy to sport is inaccurate, however, since conversation is not about winning or losing but about connectedness and elaboration. One metaphor might be animals' and children's play—which is free-form and joyful rather than structured and competitive. Another is musical improvisation in a paired or group situation—jazz being the emblematic example of what might be termed "adult play." The jazz musician has a personal style that is revealed in playing but that meshes with others in the group, much the way a good conversation reveals but mixes its participants into a lively experience. Conversation is also similar to jazz in that it risks being competitive but is, ideally, communal and elaborative of the self in concert with others.

At its best, conversation can achieve the quality of "flow"—that state of exhilaration that occurs, according to psychologist Mihaly Csikszentmihalyi, in "the delicate zone between boredom and anxiety" when concentration is focused on what is happening in the present and the participants forget everything else, including the passage of time. Csikszentmihalyi tended to associate flow with individualized creative acts, but it is also what we aspire to in conversing collegially with others.

I don't find that my conversational partners have to have the same level of education or even the same interests as I do. Montaigne and Dr. Johnson both claim that good talk can take place only between "equals," but then it depends on how equals are defined. I can sometimes converse with pleasure and ease with those who have not gone to college and feel stymied in conversation with those with multiple advanced degrees. I take "equal" to mean compatible—open, curious, and willing to engage. Readers—especially those who have read the things I like—can provide immediate kinship, but I am often surprised by people who, despite limited exposure to books, are able to articulate complex ideas that jibe with or challenge my own. The facet of character that allows for equality in conversation—and I see it as a character trait, though one that can be cultivated—is what permits a conversation to move forward.

Since conversation is, by definition, improvisational, it is always bringing to the fore new or unforeseen aspects of oneself to fit or counter or complement what the other is saying. In this way, we discover new elements in our nature as we converse. Over time, we incorporate aspects of others into ourselves in subtle and unforeseen ways (Bakhtin's "the-Other-for-me"). Initial difference from the other person seems to me fundamental to a good conversation—though difference can be relative. None of us is exactly the same or has the same opinions on things, however much we may pretend otherwise. I find it interesting that Montaigne seems to differ from the eighteenth-century satirist Jonathan Swift in welcoming "dispute" in conversation, but this may simply be a semantical distinction. Ideas that may seem disruptive or antagonistic may become interesting and fun, if presented with goodwill and patience.

One could say that in the flow of conversation the distance between self and Other is temporarily reduced—much as happens in a love relationship (indeed, as I noted, good conversation produces a feeling akin to love). It is sometimes hard to recall who said what when a conversation truly works—even when people are very different and stand ostensibly on different sides of issues.

Conversation is both a function of and a metaphor for our life in the world, always seeking to fulfill a need that is never fulfilled but whose quest gives piquancy and satisfaction, albeit temporarily and incompletely, to our encounters. In good conversation, there is always something left out, unplumbed, and unresolved, which is why we seek more of it.

CHAPTER 2

Defining and Representing Conversation

Good conversation can take various forms, and people can have different tastes in conversation. Yet certain elements seem to me to be fundamental. Here is my attempt at a definition:

> *Good conversation mixes opinions, feelings, facts, and ideas in an improvisational exchange with one or more individuals in an atmosphere of goodwill. It inspires mutual insight, respect, and, most of all, joy. It is a way of relaxing the mind, opening the heart, and connecting, authentically, with others. To converse well is surprising, humanizing, and fun.*

First and foremost, good conversation is not a chore or an exercise. It is a form of verbal sustenance—not just a seasoning to life but one of its great pleasures. And like anything precious, it is not easy to come by. As eighteenth-century poet William Cowper put it, "Words learn'd by rote a parrot may rehearse, / But talking is not always to converse." (Cowper has many excellent things to say in his long poem "Conversation," but his insights get diluted by being delivered in rhyming couplets.) Jonathan Swift, in a short work titled "Hints towards an Essay on Conversation," laments that this "so useful and innocent a pleasure, so fitted for every period and condition of life, and so much in all men's power, should be so much neglected and abused." He then proceeds to offer some rules to facilitate good conversation. I summarize these as follows: don't speak too much; don't speak inordinately about oneself; don't try too hard to be clever; don't be pedantic; don't be foolish; don't interrupt or be too concerned about being interrupted; and don't indulge in lewd or profane talk. He also advises his readers to avoid "the itch of dispute and contradiction,[the] telling of lies, or . . . the disease called the wandering of the thoughts" (i.e., excessive digression). This more or less eliminates banter, lecture, and debate (Swift, in my opinion, is being too strict with respect to the first and last of these, which, in moderate doses, can add liveliness to conversation). He also counsels against excluding women, since "a little grain of the romance is no ill ingredient to preserve and exalt the dignity of human nature, without which it is apt to degenerate into everything that is sordid, vicious, and low." The idea is admirable for the era, though we might quibble with the term "romance" for what is added to conversation when leavened by diversity of any kind. Another admonition, which strikes me as especially apt in our current moment of rampant incivility: "never say a thing which any of the company can reasonably wish we had rather left unsaid."

Swift appears to cover just about everything we *shouldn't* do in conversation but also observes, "I know few [subjects] so difficult to be treated as [they] ought, nor yet upon which there seemed so much to be said." I would translate like this: it is easier to say what one shouldn't do in conversation than to say what one should.

I would also amend Swift's last edict—"never say a thing which any of the company can reasonably wish we had rather left unsaid"—in positive terms: "*Be sure to frame any contro-versial idea that you wish to share in such a way that it will not offend.*"

What is described here is, of course, easier said than done. Even the most devoted and practiced conversationalists will occasionally find themselves devolve into conformist chatter, covert competitiveness, or outright conflict. These are the ene-mies of conversation and yet are inevitable at times, given the nature of human beings and the resentments and conditioned responses that can flair up in us without warning. And what if what we want to say is potentially offensive? Can we always say what we mean without giving offense in such circumstances?

I should explain at this point that I am speaking of conversa-tion as a kind of Platonic ideal. Anthropologist Gregory Bate-son, one of my favorite thinkers, included a series of conversa-tions with his young daughter in his brilliant collection of essays, *Steps to an Ecology of Mind*; he describes these as focused on "some problematic subject" in which "the structure of the conversation is also relevant to the same subject." I do believe that the form-follows-function aspect of these "Metalogues," as he calls them, is what happens in the best conversations. When I teach Shakespeare, for example, I sometimes marvel at how the class has duplicated the paradoxes in the plays in the way their comments unfold.

I know that most of the time, I do not approach this kind of profound, organically integrated exchange, what I like to call "sublime conversation" and which Dr. Johnson referred to, less extravagantly, as "solid conversation." I often find it hard to con-verse even moderately well, no less achieve the ideal I have in mind. Still, I hold out for this ideal because I have on occasion approached it and know that it is worth aspiring to. I remain convinced that, with practice and when the conversants and the setting align, it is possible to engage on a range of topics, even very difficult ones, with sincerity, civility, and joy.

I also believe that even the most mundane and brief exchanges can contain germs of the ideal and be replenishing. I recently had a conversation with the manager of the hotel where I was staying about her care for the flowers in the lobby. The discussion, which began with my praise of the hydrangeas that had remained fresh over a four-day stay, moved into a discussion of our mutual love of flowers, the varieties we like best, how we care for them, and their fleeting beauty. The conversation, lasting no more than ten minutes, was as delightful and uplifting as the gift of a bouquet.

That said, when I speak of conversation in this book, I mostly speak of it as something more sustained, probing, and challenging in nature, although not without moments of humor and lightness. This is what Stephen Miller in his excellent *Conversation: A History of a Declining Art* refers to (citing philosopher Michael Oakeshott) as "an unrehearsed intellectual adventure." Such conversation is particularly worth practicing at the present moment when our dealings with each other seem so fraught and acrimonious.

Lessons in argument and persuasion go back to antiquity, but this period also practiced non-utilitarian conversation of the sort I value most. Roman philosopher and rhetorician Marcus Tullius Cicero is perhaps the most notable classical figure to address the topic. In his *Treatise on Friendship*, he extols the joy of speaking uninhibitedly with people you trust: "What can be more delightful than to have someone to whom you can say everything with the same absolute confidence as to yourself?" One could argue that Cicero was the first to see conversation as an end in itself as well as an instructive or persuasive activity.

During the Renaissance, the topic was taken up by several commentators, including Baldassieri Castiglione, who in *The Book of the Courtier* presents his views as a series of dialogues that stress diplomacy, graciousness, and subtle manipulation toward a given end. Castiglione's focus on the instrumental aspect of conversation makes him a kind of Renaissance version of twentieth-century guides to getting ahead.

The great essayist Montaigne wrote extensively on conversation in its purer form, extolling it as necessary to his well-being: "If I were now compelled to choose, I should sooner, I think, consent to lose my sight, than my hearing and speech," he wrote in his essay on the subject. He repeats almost verbatim the statement by Cicero about the unburdening aspect of conversation: "How can life be worth living . . . which lacks that repose which is to be found in the mutual good will of a friend? What can be more delightful than to have someone to whom you can say everything with the same absolute confidence as yourself?" One feels the pathos of this statement, given that Montaigne lost his most cherished friend, Étienne de la Boétie, at an early age and never ceased to mourn that loss.

Having presumably had an ideal conversationalist in his deceased friend, Montaigne seems to be especially critical when people fail to converse properly. One of my favorites of his admonitions comes from his essay "Of Pedantry": "Like birds who fly abroad to forage for grain and bring it home in the beak, without tasting it themselves, to feed their young; so our pedants go picking here and there, out of books, and hold it at the tongue's end, only to spit it out and distribute it abroad." I will forever retain the image, spurred by this description, of a particular colleague spitting out nuggets of sententiousness to anyone who would listen.

The eighteenth century was a great age for conversation, and Dr. Johnson, Jonathan Swift, Oliver Goldsmith, David Hume, Joseph Addison, and Henry Fielding are among the British authors of the period to provide commentary on what they considered to be important for good talk, mostly focusing on the "don'ts"—with digression, pretentiousness, and boastfulness singled out as conversational detriments. In eighteenth-century America, Benjamin Franklin outlined six rules for conversation in his 1748 *Poor Richard Improved*: avoid flattery, be a good listener, be open to new ideas, avoid trying to be too witty, have a sense of humor, and answer to the purpose. George Washington wrote 114 rules for polite conversation when he was fourteen years old and, as a general, was known for being an excellent listener (the same was said for another general, Dwight D. Eisenhower). A recent book on the founders makes the point that the American Revolution was successful, mobilizing disparate people to its cause, as a result of long and probing conversation among constituents across the colonies. The British, by contrast, were fated to lose the war because George III refused to listen to, no less converse with, his American subjects.

In the nineteenth century, especially in America when shaping the self alongside shaping the country became something of a national obsession, conversation of the more instrumental variety was one of the activities that an aspiring gentleman could work to improve. We see the publication of numerous etiquette books with titles like *Manners for Men, Manual for Politeness, Social Life, and Hints on Etiquette*, and *Usages of Society with a Glance at Bad Habits*—all of which give guidance on conversation. The most esteemed work on the subject was the 1887 *Principles of the Art of Conversation* by J. P. Mahaffy, who gives instructions on such issues as how to deal constructively with physical impediments (a slight stammer, he notes, can add piquancy to conversation), the need for both general and specialized knowledge, the way to improve intellectual quickness (by being around people who are intellectually quick), the value of moral qualities like modesty, simplicity, and sympathy (but not to the point of "gushing"), as well as the importance of avoiding shyness ("a social crime"), selfishness, impatience, and interruption. People who talk too much, he notes,

> kill more conversation than they create, nor do they understand that the very meaning of the word implies a contribution-feast, an *eranos* as the Greeks would say, not the entertainment provided by a single host. But alas! In a lesser and looser sense these people often dominate society for years, and are even sought out as social conveniences, who will keep things going at a dinner table, and supply the defects of silence and dullness so painfully common in English more than in other societies.

Mahaffy has a lot in his book that seems to me astute and, in many respects, modern in substance if not in style.

In the twentieth century, the most notable figure in conversational self-help was Dale Carnegie, who created an entire industry out of teaching aspiring social and business climbers based on his most famous book, *How to Win Friends and Influence People.* Carnegie began writing and giving courses in the 1920s, and his business survived him to grow into an empire today ("over 200 offices in 85 countries") with supporting textbooks, online resources, newsletters, and blogs; their tag line: "Training options that transform your impact." The message dovetails with the American myth of upward mobility and getting ahead through grit and self-improvement, encapsulated in the late nineteenth-century Horatio Alger stories and parodied in the mid-twentieth-century musical *How to Succeed in Business without Really Trying*.

The self-improvement programs of Dale Carnegie have an offshoot in the self-realization movement of the past few decades. A deluge of books in recent years link conversational skills to less careerist, more creative and relational goals. Given the upscale demographic for this kind of self-help, one could argue that it represents the follow-up to Carnegie: helping people find fulfillment after they've made it in business and found that it doesn't give them the unmitigated happiness they sought. Still, books like Leil Lowndes's *How to Talk to Anyone: 92 Little Tricks for Big Success in Relationship* and Sarah Rozenthuler's *How to Have Meaningful Conversations: 7 Strategies for Talking about What Matters* provide rules not very different from those laid out by books about conversation from earlier periods.

Some recent works like Sherry Turkle's *Reclaiming Conversation: The Power of Talk in a Digital Age* lament how the internet has hurt the art of conversation. Others try to distinguish good conversation from argument and debate and to school us in more civil encounters, like William Isaacs's *Dialogue: The Art of Thinking Together*. Several are eloquent apologias for conversation that trace its history, like Catherine Blyth's *The Art of Conversation: A Guided Tour of a Neglected Pleasure* and Miller's *Conversation: A History of a Declining Art*, already mentioned.

Having surveyed the abundant publications on conversation over this century and last, I find myself particularly charmed by a short but entertaining 1936 work, *The Art of Conversation*, by Milton Wright. The book is full of citations from philosophy and literature, with thumbnail sketches about "the ancient symposia" and the "talkers of Old England" while also containing exhaustive descriptions of conversational scenarios. In one case, the author describes a wife explaining to her husband how he should converse over dinner with his client about his love of fishing and pipe smoking (Wright gives a verbatim account of the wife practicing the conversation in advance of the dinner); another in which the author explains his personal research into how a homely girl has become popular with men by asking many questions and making them feel important and knowledgeable. In a chapter on "developing repartee" he gives minute instruction on how to come up with a clever thought and insert it into conversation, advising, "It must be prompt. It must be impromptu. It must be based upon the same premise that called it forth. It must outshine the original remark." The author advises practicing imaginary scenarios so as not to suffer *l'esprit d'escalier* (carefully defined for the reader: "you think of the scintillating remarks you could have made back there if only you had thought of them"). The book has sections on "using flattery," "seeking an opinion," and "let him parade his talents."

The book's erudition combined with its unadorned acknowledgment of human vanity is astounding, and yet the tone is entirely upbeat and lacking in cynicism—a masterpiece of the American pragmatic spirit at its most naïve early in the twentieth century as the country began to gain prominence on the world stage. It is perhaps no coincidence that Wright reminds me of Castiglione and Machiavelli in his tone; they too were writing at a high point of their civilization, were astute about human nature but optimistic about how the individual could rise through deliberate study and strategy. And yet, even as Wright explains the levers by which one can manipulate others to become a "successful" conversationalist, he ends on a surprisingly moving note that undercuts his own lessons: "If you can forget yourself, then you have learned the innermost secret of the art of good conversation. All the rest is a matter of technique."

I love this book for its unabashed willingness to put forward this contradiction. One can make one's conversation better by following certain instructions about listening well and employing certain opening gambits, transitions, and techniques for putting one's partner at ease; one may even practice "repartee" as Wright suggests. But the secret to conversation, "forgetting oneself," cannot be taught. It is akin to the double bind that psychologists refer to when someone tells us to "be spontaneous." The admonition goes against the grain of what is involved—a state of being that happens by being swept up in the "flow" of the moment.

This brings me to the major point I want to cover in this chapter. If the flow of conversation cannot be fully willed or taught, neither can it be fully *represented*. Interestingly, the elusive side to life has become a topic of analysis these days among the proponents of "affect theory." They try to take into account the emotional and subjective elements in culture that can shape our thinking and behavior. Much of the affective turn in cultural studies has concentrated on the negative side of this process, the way our feelings can be manipulated to work against the social good and our own self-interest. But in "sublime conversation" there is a positive affect that happens between or among people that escapes representation. We can compare this to the impossibility of representing in writing a piece of music or a painting, though the challenge with conversation is also different. It is a matter of translating not from one medium to another but from one state of being to another. Just as it is impossible to measure the position of an electron without changing that position, when we tape or film or even overhear a conversation, we are missing its vital, experiential aspect. (Okay, the analogy is not quite apt—electrons don't have feelings.)

Some filmmakers attempt to evoke the "feel" of conversation with varying degrees of success. Those who try for realism in this regard seem to me to fall short (I'm thinking of the use of overlapping dialogue in Robert Altman's films, for example, which I find headache-inducing). One representation that strikes me as insightful without pretending to realism occurs in the 1981 movie *My Dinner with André*. When the film debuted, it was an art house hit, and being young and intellectually impressionable at the time, I felt I should like it. Yet, quite frankly, I was bored and couldn't figure out what the movie was trying to do. Recently, I watched it again in the context of thinking about conversation for this book, and the effect was entirely different. I could see that the film was trying to anatomize what happens in good conversation.

The film has a progressive structure, which, by definition, runs counter to reality. Inside a good conversation, we don't feel we are going anywhere in particular; we enter the "flow" or, in Milton Wright's terms, we forget ourselves. But this is cinematic representation, and by definition, it is tied to a dramatic structure.

The following is an analysis of the film that explains what I think it is up to.

It begins with the playwright and actor Wallace Shawn on his way to meet his friend, the director André Gregory, for dinner. One of the elements that makes this movie interesting is that these actors are playing themselves, and the line between the reality of what they do and say and the representation for the sake of cinematic structure is intentionally blurred.

Wally (as André will call him) is speaking in voice-over as we watch him hurry through New York City on his way to the restaurant that André has chosen for them to meet. There is a shot of an overstuffed garbage can as he approaches the crowded subway he will take to his destination, images that underline the

character's straitened circumstances. Although André was responsible for launching Wally's still-tenuous playwrighting
career, he tells us in the voice-over that he is dreading their
meeting. He hasn't seen his friend for some years and has heard
that André has become increasingly eccentric and detached
from the theater scene.

When Wally enters the restaurant, which is elegant and apparently expensive, he seems out of place in his shabby clothes
and schlubby demeanor. Having arrived first, he is directed to
the ornate bar where he is soon joined by André, who is entirely
at home and knows the waiters. They are seated at a beautifully
set table, and André begins talking almost at once. What follows for the next half hour or so is a practical soliloquy, interrupted only by the food being ordered and served. André describes his travels and his exotic experiences in quest of
fulfillment and illumination. Wally, who has already told us in
voice-over that "asking questions always relaxes me," interjects
with short queries, adding an occasional "hmm" or "I see" to
André's long, meandering, fantastical narrative. One thing is
clear at this point: this is not a conversation but a surreal sort of
exposition. At first, it has a mild fascination but soon comes to
seem boring and silly. We sense that Wally feels the same way,
even as he urges his friend to go on.

Finally, halfway or so through the film, Wally begins to say
more, agreeing at first with some part of what André says, but
then pushing back at his friend's solipsism and assumption that,
without exotic travel and experience, life is meaningless and
without fulfillment. He takes the position of the little man finding solace and joy in small, everyday occurrences, and seems to
speak in counterpoint to the clearly privileged André, who has
surfeited on the pleasures and opportunities that have been

afforded him. More specifically, Wally espouses science and the scientific method as basic to his belief in contrast to the zany spirituality of André.

This might be a point of stasis—in which the characters become aligned against each other and harden into classist stereotypes. But the genius of the film—or rather, of the characters as they represent themselves—is their ability to move beyond this into a true conversation, listening intently to each other and eventually finding points of overlap and agreement about the theater, relationships, and the meaning of life. André is not angry or resentful at Wally's initial critical response; he tries to meet it on its own terms, agreeing in part but also elaborating on his own position in such a way that Wally can also agree with him.

The movie is full of ideas, but it also has something of the patina of farce—it is outlandish, both in the stories that André tells and in the mannerisms and expressions of Wally (and the old waiter who serves them dinner). This is absurdist theater even as it is a deliberate and a highly intellectual model for how conversation might, in a dramatized way, unfurl.

I should note that soon after I drafted this chapter, an article appeared in the *New York Times* revisiting the film and calling it "the original podcast." This is to overlook the highly artful nature of its making. It seems that Shawn and Gregory had taped conversations together over a period of time from which Shawn created the script for the movie that, in turn, was directed by French director Louis Malle. In short, it is not a real conversation but a staged one, another production by the two men who, as they discuss at certain points, have collaborated in the past.

Detractors have argued that the film is a failure because a movie is supposed to move and that talk is, by definition, visually static. But the clash of form (talk vs. moving image) is larger than this; it involves the fact that conversation cannot be fully experienced except in real time when we are inside of it. What *My Dinner with André* does is *evoke* a real conversation as it evolves out of a monologue. This, to my mind, is the best we can do if we want to represent rather than actually engage in conversation. And perhaps this is the point. The very act of representing or even of overhearing conversation turns the thing into a performance, gives it a mannered, if not a farcical aspect.

It may seem at times that we are surrounded by conversation—on talk shows, TV panels, interviews, YouTube clips, and podcasts. The image of pundits seated at a table dissecting an event in the news can be found at any hour of the day—or night (if one happens to have insomnia as I do). But these are rarely true conversations, only variations on predetermined positions, with each participant given a small allotment of time to provide a "sound bite." The term is antithetical to the idea of conversation, though it is often all that is left of a potential conversation, like the carcass of a chicken that others have eaten. One might think that cable news shows with their twenty-four-hour cycles would have more time for substantive talk, but these stations are devoted to political positions where nuance might leave an opening for critics to attack. The rehashing of the same topics in the same way by the same people is also cheaper to produce and intellectually easier to perform. Zoom talk, initiated during the pandemic but here to stay, has introduced another variable: even seemingly private or confidential conversations can be hacked and recorded without the knowledge of the participants and made available to a wide audience. This has made conversation on Zoom more deliberate even when it is not formally recorded, since we never know who is listening in or surreptitiously transcribing what is being said.

One of the dangers of so much conversation of a staged and highly predictable sort is that it makes it more difficult for people to pursue genuine conversation in private space. They learn to fall back on what they have seen modeled on TV or online; they resort to clichéd language and uninflected positions on issues. In our performance-saturated culture where people feel they are always on display, it is easier and safer to take refuge in prescribed expression. Milton Wright's scenarios in his 1936 book have a certain force and originality because he was writing before television and before media trainers began to manipulate how politicians and other public figures express themselves.

People say that the famous television debate between Nixon and Kennedy was a turning point in political life: Kennedy took advantage of the visual nature of the medium to achieve victory (those who listened to the debate on the radio thought that Nixon had won). But the real turning point, in my view, came more than twenty years later during the presidency of Ronald Reagan, who pioneered the "art" (so to speak) of curated talk. Reagan created a highly controlled self-presentation that *sounded* conversational. He was known to turn statements into questions and to insert colloquialisms and contractions in place of more formal speech. The effect was disarming, even to those who opposed his policies. I recall listening to him and admitting that I liked the man, though precisely what it was I liked was hard to say. His speech was platitudinous but somehow intimate and soothing in tone. Reagan also pioneered a disciplined PR strategy: a "line of the day" and a "message of the week" that informed everything he (and his staff) said to the press and the public. This flies in the face of the serendipity and spontaneity that characterize real conversation. It may well be that Reagan's example, through its extraordinary success and superficial appeal, debased political conversation—and beyond that, all conversation—more thoroughly than any other figure in history.

And yet, human beings, being what they are, occasionally break through the performance, often in unseemly ways, given the repression that has been put in place. Jeffrey Toobin, who during a break in a Zoom brainstorming session with his New Yorker colleagues was caught masturbating on screen, seems a commentary on the way the tension associated with a relentlessly predictable public face may lead to the literal need for release behind the scenes. The contrast between the superarticulate Anthony Weiner and the fact that he sent pictures of his genitalia to women on the internet suggests a similar kind of duality. Both men suffered, one might hypothesize, from an absence of the sort of intimacy that comes with genuine interaction. Freud, in his late work *Civilization and Its Discontents*, predicted this sort of behavior. He felt that the repressive demands of society were too great and that this would lead to neurotic acting out (e.g., masturbation online or sending unseemly pix to strangers).

Perhaps to ease this kind of strain, many presidents have felt the need for private conversation, unconnected to their public role. John and Jackie Kennedy held informal gatherings at the White House during their administration in which they conversed with people who they felt would be intellectually interesting. Bill Clinton was presumably a great conversationalist and could talk late into the night with colleagues and friends. Barack Obama invited writers he admired to converse with him. Yet though we get reports of these conversations, even snippets or transcripts of what was said, we cannot know what they were actually like, not being part of them or even present to catch the tone. I have heard, on the one hand, that Clinton was a great conversationalist; on the other, that he tended to monopolize any gathering with his indefatigable talk. Perhaps it depended on who he was talking to. (The same could be said about Coleridge, who some found enthralling, others garrulously tedious.)

If conversation is a metaphor for life, it is also part of life and, as such, fully available only through lived experience and dependent on the existence of a certain ineffable compatibility that certain people have for each other.

CHAPTER 3

Food, Drink, and Conversation

It's hard to say which form of nourishment, food or drink, better supports conversation. Obviously, they work best together, but there are certain advantages to a bar, which Dr. Johnson referred to as "the throne of human felicity"—whether a grungy grad student joint where friends meet after class or a ritzier gathering place with leather backs to the seats and a polished mahogany surface that offers a sense of luxe and comfort. Having outgrown the former, I prefer the latter, where I can generally count on the bartender's not smirking when I order a "weak whiskey sour, on the sweet side."

A bar has the advantage of serendipity. It is one of the few places where one can start a conversation with a complete stranger. There is also the fact of being able to easily extricate oneself from a bar conversation (you can finish your drink and leave, which is less possible at a dinner that has to move through a set of prescribed courses).

People sometimes say that the noise and distraction of a bar is not conducive to conversation, and too much noise can certainly be distracting. I have been at weddings and bar mitzvahs where one has to literally scream above the din of the band or DJ. Very quickly, everyone gives up on conversation and surrenders to frenetic dancing, a state of stricken silence, or a retreat to the bathrooms where older guests try to converse as the teenagers apply lip gloss in the mirror.

On the other hand, a bar, with a hum in the background, even an old-fashioned jukebox playing in the corner, can be just what one wants to jump-start a conversation. A certain kind of hubbub creates a sense that one's words do not carry too much weight; they blend easily into the general ambience. There is also something to be said for having to push gently against the background noise, to work with resistance, so to speak, so as to make one's conversation take on more importance and forcefulness (one's tolerance for such resistance does seem to decrease with age).

A well-stocked bar is in itself an incitement to conversation, especially if one has a modicum of interest in vintages or single malts. Nothing is a better conversation starter than whether the stranger beside you prefers Glenfiddich to Macallan, a segue into the fact that you both have taken distillery tours in Scotland or like the whiskey coming out of Japan.

Unfortunately, a single woman is always subject to scrutiny at a bar. Jonathan Swift noted that women help conversation, but he presents this idea in the context of "romance." Romance here may be a euphemism for flirtation and can escalate into harassment. At a bar, there is the pressure to flirt that can lead to bristling when your conversant seems too bent on amorous attention. I am not against friendly flirtation—I believe it adds spice to conversation and, in its most subtle form, is endemic to playful interaction with both men and women. But overt and aggressive flirtation has a tendency to be smarmy and slide into abuse. Our current society has become more aware of this, which tends to make it less of a problem—men claim to be terrified of a misstep, but such claims can erode quickly after a few drinks. My recent experience with mannerly men in bars may be the result of my advancing age and the fact that I am rarely there without my husband beside me. Even if he is disinclined to talk with the computer security analyst with whom I have struck up a conversation ("I could hack your bank account in twenty minutes if I wanted to"), his tacit presence beside me keeps the hacker at bay.

Though some women may object, I feel obliged to report that a bar is more a precinct for male conversation, often with the bartender, a classic trope in romantic movies: the lovelorn male lead confiding in the hardened but sympathetic bartender. The emblematic rendering is in Frank Sinatra's 1949 "One for My Baby (And One More for the Road)." My friend Fred Abbate, sadly no longer with us, used to love certain hotel bars where the bartenders knew to bring him an Old Bushmills on the rocks and where he would expound on Aristotle to those within hearing. Fred had a PhD in philosophy and assumed that everyone was as interested in Aristotle as he was—and given his exceptional gift for conversation (helped by the Old Bushmills), he convinced them they were.

While I have had a few random, surprising encounters and some fun chats with colleagues after work, I can hardly say that bars have afforded me prolonged and deep talk of the sort that I equate with the best kind of conversation. For that, I favor the sit-down meal. Philosopher Emmanuel Levinas argued on behalf of the civilizing role of food in separating the nonhuman from the human: "Food is not the fuel necessary to the human machine. Food is a meal." This "meal," in my view, is where food (and drink) are eaten in leisurely fashion, and conversation takes place with people who are eager to engage collegially with each other.

My favorite representation of a meal as it encourages the best sort of conversation occurs in Virginia Woolf's 1929 *A Room of*

One's Own. The work, which is taught in women's studies courses around the world, began its life as a lecture to the women's colleges of Girton and Newnham at Cambridge University at a time when the colleges that made up Oxford and Cambridge were segregated by sex. In the lecture-turned-essay, Woolf creates an alter ego for herself in the narrating character who pays a visit to "Oxbridge University," a fictional composite of the two great bastions of British elite education. She takes her lunch and dinner at a male and a female college, respectively, within this fictional Oxbridge.

The centerpiece of the first part of the essay and, to my mind, the most compelling passage in the work, is the luncheon that the narrator attends at the male college. There is some elaborate buildup to this event, making clear that the setting is exclusive and supported by great wealth. But I will jump to the crux of the matter, the meal itself (edited slightly for the sake of efficient reading):

> The lunch on this occasion began with soles, sunk in a deep dish, over which the college cook had spread a counterpane of the whitest cream, save that it was branded here and there with brown spots like the spots on the flanks of a doe. After that came the partridges, but if this suggests a couple of bald, brown birds on a plate you are mistaken. The partridges, many and various, came with all their retinue of sauces and salads, the sharp and the sweet, each in its order; their potatoes, thin as coins but not so hard; their sprouts, foliated as rosebuds but more succulent. And no sooner had the roast and its retinue been done with than the silent serving man . . . set before us, wreathed in napkins, a confection which rose all sugar from the waves. To call it pudding and so relate it to rice and tapioca would be an insult. Meanwhile the wine-

glasses had flushed yellow and flushed crimson: had been emptied; had been filled. And thus by degrees was lit, half-way down the spine, which is the seat of the soul, not the hard little electric light which we call brilliance, as it pops in and out upon our lips, but the more profound, subtle and subterranean glow, which is the rich yellow flame of rational intercourse. No need to hurry. No need to sparkle. No need to be anybody but oneself.

This is an extraordinary passage—a paeon to food and drink of the best sort, but more, to how such nourishment can facilitate good talk. This is, to be sure, a specific kind of conversation, what Dr. Johnson referred to as "solid"—neither mundane chit-chat nor erudite academic discussion but, in Woolf's eloquent phrase, "the rich yellow flame of rational intercourse," an exchange where there is "No need to hurry. No need to sparkle. No need to be anybody but oneself." In other words, one can be honest but receptive; open, tolerant, modest, and thoughtful—"oneself" or, more correctly, "one's best self." I would also characterize the emergence of this best self as the result of "forgetting oneself" in the *flow* of conversation, in Milton Wright's phrase. It has affinities, I think, with what Romantic poet John Keats called "negative capability"—a comfort with contradiction and ambiguity that feels no need for rigorous, scientific proof (though Keats, like Csikszentmihalyi with his idea of "flow," was thinking primarily of solitary artistic creation).

One reason why I am so taken by this passage from *A Room of One's Own* is because it evokes my own experience in one of the first classes of women to be admitted to an elite college, an American Oxbridge, in 1971. During my time in that place, which seemed magical to my eighteen-year-old self, there was nothing I looked forward to more than entering the neo-Gothic dining hall with its enormous portraits of venerable professors (of course, all white and male) to survey the menu of the day and the people already seated at the wooden tables with whom I would share it. The food was copious, varied, and well-prepared (at least to my suburban palate—my mother, though an excellent storyteller, was a pedestrian cook), and I firmly believe that, following Woolf, it helped to inspire the quality of talk we engaged in: rational intercourse of a high order. Ideas were traded with abandon, nothing was off-limits, devil's advocate positions assumed with relish. No one was aware of being incorrect or untoward. An unfair or mean-spirited remark would be called out, but its perpetrator was not banished or stigmatized for all eternity. The meals were meant to be places where ideas were expressed in uninhibited fashion and where it was easy to forgive slights or reflexive blindnesses. I am convinced that the kind of conversation we engaged in over good food in that dining hall did more to raise the consciousness of the bigot and broaden the outlook of the chemistry major than any amount of diversity training would have done.

In *My Dinner with André*, discussed in the previous chapter, it is the comfortable, beautifully appointed restaurant setting and the leisurely arrival of well-prepared courses that help bring these two very different people into what eventually is an exhilarating and uplifting exchange. Wally is at first ill at ease in the opulent setting, but it eventually seems to create a comfortable, "safe" space where he can be fully himself and heard and, finally, can make possible a synthesis of his and André's ideas. The fact that he orders an amaretto with his expresso at the end of the meal (by his own inclination and not inspired by André, who orders only an expresso) seems to mark the point when he has begun to feel at ease in this gracious setting, when the sumptuous food and wine have done their work. After he leaves the

restaurant, he "treats" himself to a taxi home, and the overriding
feeling communicated to the audience is one of contentment,
even joy, at the achievement of a connection between himself
and the friend whom he had originally dreaded seeing.

Woolf makes the point that the kind of food served at the
Oxbridge luncheon, that I experienced in college and that Wally
was served in his dinner with André, requires wealth—one's
own or someone else's to subsidize it. Woolf brings this point
home when, the same day that she takes the sumptuous luncheon at the men's college, she goes to dinner at the fictional
women's college down the road. It is clear, right way, that her
intention is to mark a stark and important difference between
the two meals. Here is her description of the dinner at the
women's college:

Dinner was ready. Here was the soup. It was a plain gravy
soup. There was nothing to stir the fancy in that. One could
have seen through the transparent liquid any pattern that
there might have been on the plate itself. But there was no
pattern. The plate was plain. Next came beef with its atten-
dant greens and potatoes—a homely trinity, suggesting the
rumps of cattle in a muddie market, and sprouts curled and
yellowed at the edge, and bargaining and cheapening, and
women with string bags on Monday morning. There was no
reason to complain of human nature's daily food, seeing that
the supply was sufficient and coal-miners doubtless were sitting down to less. Prunes and custard followed. And if any
one complains that prunes, even when mitigated by custard,
are an uncharitable vegetable (fruit they are not), stringy as
a miser's heart and exuding a fluid such as might run in mi-
sers' veins who have denied themselves wine and warmth for
eighty years and yet not given to the poor, he should reflect

that there are people whose charity embraces even the prune. Biscuits and cheese came next, and here the water-jug was liberally passed round, for it is the nature of biscuits to be dry, and these were biscuits to the core. That was all. The meal was over.

This is very funny but also very sad. Woolf knows how to make her point about women's status in culture and about what is lost when elements that seem like negligible frills are missing. One may quarrel with the extreme manner in which Woolf writes: the lush descriptive language for the luncheon; the curt, often adjective-less sentences with their crude ironic asides for the dinner. One may quibble with her traducing of prunes (which I happen to like). But the point is made, and she brings it home succinctly at the end of the passage about the women's dinner:

> Conversation for a moment flagged. The human frame being what it is, heart body and brain all mixed together, and not contained in separate compartments as they will be no doubt in another million years, a good dinner is of great importance to good talk. One cannot think well, love well, sleep well, if one has not dined well. The lamp in the spine does not light on beef and prunes.

The men's college is rich and can provide the kind of repast that encourages conversation. The women's college is poor, and its bare-bones dinner does not encourage conversation, at least in the form that is most pleasant and conducive to ease and spontaneity; that is, to the exercise, as it were, of one's best self.

We are reminded that the meager fare of the women's table is better than what many others in society must eat. Woolf's sense of the relativity of want is alive and well. But for all that coal miners and others less fortunate dine less well, the issue is not nourishment but engagement. Deprivation, she implies, may be conducive to genius; she notes pointedly that the splendid luncheon at the male college does not inspire brilliant *bon mots*; one might even argue that people in want are spurred to create at a higher level than those afforded every luxury. But even if this is the case (and I'm not sure that it is or that Woolf believes that it is), it does so at the expense of the soul (one's best self). It does not afford the pleasure that the soul takes in the ease, cheer, and fellowship that good food and drink inspire.

When administrators or bottom-line-oriented trustees at universities see increased outlays for the dining hall as a waste of money, they miss the larger point that this is useful in getting students to relax, commune, and trade ideas. Good food is a civilizing force, an insurance policy against insurrection. How can we really be angry with each other over excellent roast chicken, a baked potato with sour cream, and a make-your-own sundae? And this is the mundane fare that will placate anyone. Take it up a notch—beef Wellington, salmon *en croute*, oysters Rockefeller, marron glacé—such fare not only feeds the palate but creates mental curiosity and subject matter for discussion. Mussels marinara involve some degree of effort and concentration, not to mention a certain amount of curiosity from the uninitiated that is in itself a civilizing, intellectual force. When I became dean of the Honors College at my university, I asked a previous dean, who happens also to be a good friend and something of a gastronome, the secret to his success in leading and building the program. He replied, "Food. It is important to have it at all events, and make it as plentiful and good as possible." I have heeded that advice, and any event we sponsored (prior to COVID-19) always included the notation "refreshments will be served."

Food provides both predictable continuity and a sense of expectation and surprise. If one goes to a movie, a concert, a play, or a museum with friends, the experience is invariably supplemented by what one of my friends calls "delayed conversation"—the sense that we will recess afterward for a meal in which the experience will be discussed and other ideas brought to the table. I understand the French tendency to draw out a meal into multiple courses: the salad served separately (generally after the entrée), then the cheese course, the dessert, and the coffee followed by the after-dinner drink or *digestif*. On the one occasion in my life when I had dinner at a two-star Michelin restaurant, what I most recall is not the food but the superbly orchestrated presentation of the courses, the impeccable service, and the general sense of well-being that made my husband's conversation, always rather good, seem unusually delightful and clever. After all, how could it be anything but, as we nibbled on the last of a perfect *tarte tatin*, having finished off the cheese plate with its sliver of blue, havarti, and brie, its dollop of fig jam and cluster of grapes?

By the same token, it is also possible to take issue with Virginia Woolf's depiction of a division that connects good conversation to the copiousness and quality of the food. Although I obviously love good food and feel that it and good drink aid conversation, I also know that some of the best conversations I've had have been in more mundane locales over a hamburger (before I gave up eating meat) or a cheese sandwich (after). Woolf's depiction of her dinner at the women's college is one of monastic asceticism, but add a tablecloth and flowers, dim the lights, and contribute some comfortable chairs, and the whole scene could well mutate into something far more congenial. What the women's college suffers from more than poverty is a sense of being comparatively poor—of being "less" than its male counterpart. Good food is a stimulant to conversation, but it is also a symbol of ease, tolerance, and plenty. A sense of belonging and being cared for encourages camaraderie and conversation. A sense of being marginalized and diminished in the eyes of others is an obstacle to it.

We are now in a foodie culture, and some of my friends (though more often the children of my friends—this seems to be a trend among the younger set, especially in New York City) are up on the latest restaurants and will spend an inordinate amount of money on a meal that promises to be exceptional. An antiques dealer in my neighborhood recently addressed this trend. She said that she was going out of business because young people buy food more than they buy "things" (antiques, objets d'art), which used to draw them in the past.

By the same token, there is a great deal to be said for the predictable eating establishment, where you care less for the quality of food than for the camaraderie and conversation. I recently heard a discussion on the radio about the merits of diners where you know exactly what to expect. I have had some of the most delightful conversations in diners—especially when desert comes around and my friends and I decide to share a piece of gargantuan chocolate cake.

A restaurant meal is particularly conducive to conversation because the chores attached to preparing and serving (not to mention cleaning up) are eliminated. The novelty of the atmosphere can also jog us to relax our guard and think and respond more creatively. A child psychologist once told me that the best way to encourage conversation with a teenager is to take her to a restaurant for a one-on-one meal. I have found that conversing with my children in the car also works—the space is neutral, and they cannot escape to their room—but a restaurant is better because it adds the pleasure and diversion of food and incorporates the ordering and serving that can help punctuate the conversation and give time for the mental digestion of ideas.

I have not addressed drink as an aid to conversation. I mentioned that a bar can be a good but limited site, but there is no denying that drink as an accompaniment to a meal will help it taste better and make the participants relax and enjoy themselves more. Scientists say that drink in moderation supports the "flow" of creativity, but move beyond moderation and it inhibits. The problem, of course, is defining moderation, and that can swing wildly from one drink to a bottle of wine—or two. So much depends on individual tolerance and custom. I grew up in a Jewish culture where food was pushed on everyone, but alcohol aroused modest terror. If my father came home from a hard day at work and poured himself two fingers of scotch, my mother was sure he was on his way to being a "Bowery bum" (a phrase that may have fallen out of use, though the image of my father, lying in the street, clutching a whiskey bottle in a brown paper bag remains alive in my imagination of disaster to this day).

America, as one author notes, has traditionally had a dichotomous relationship to drink, supporting excess drinking in some quarters and eras, and total abstention in others. This contrasts the French and Southern Europeans who have always incorporated drink into their culture and rarely drink to get drunk. The accompaniment of wine at lunch and dinner, beginning in toddlerhood (the only age when the French allow wine to be watered down), may account for why the people of that nation are such good conversationalists. Recent evidence suggests that alcohol may have predated bread and helped to jump-start civilization. Study after study show that people who drink moderately with others (as opposed to alone) are happier than those who abstain entirely. (I will discuss the special case of the drinking culture on the college campus in chapter 9.)

I find it interesting to observe how fashion in alcohol mutates as the culture changes. Specialty cocktails, which were popular in the *Mad Men* fifties, seemed vulgar and bourgeois in the seventies and eighties but have come back into vogue at even modest restaurants nowadays. Cocktails are, indeed, useful as the launching pad for the meal and for conversation; they both prolong the period at the table and set a lively, festive tone for what follows.

Sustainability has now become a major issue at the dinner table as elsewhere, and more and more people are vegetarians or vegans. But the quality of food that can be created within these strictures is also impressive—and the fact of such tastes and concerns, not to mention the preparation entailed to accommodate them, is, in itself, great fodder for conversation. I find the issue of what we should or shouldn't eat and how animals should be raised for food endlessly fascinating and instructive of larger issues in our culture.

While I do believe that conversation can proceed over modest meals and that fine food is associated with a life of privilege, this does not mean that it should be jettisoned as too elitist any more than opera, ballet, or classical music should be shunned for attracting a privileged audience. Instead, we need to find a way to make exceptional food, like great art and culture, available to more people, not for physical sustenance, where plain soup, beef, and vegetables will do just fine, but for mental sustenance, to pique curiosity and enlarge experience, and thereby to help people engage with each other more expansively.

The idea of food as a means of softening and rounding out ideas is hardly new. Meals have always been central to diplomatic encounters among heads of state and diplomatic envoys. One of the best scenes in the Netflix series *The Crown* involves Princess Margaret meeting with Lyndon Johnson and finding common ground (and a resolution to a sticking point in American-British financial relations) as they share drinks and dinner, imbibing and eating with great gusto, trading dirty limericks and jabs at the late president Kennedy. (It strikes me as an interesting coincidence that here, at Woolf's Oxbridge luncheon, and in *My Dinner with André*, the main course is partridge or squab; perhaps these game birds are uniquely suited to inciting lively conversation!). It is said that the scene with President Johnson and Princess Margaret does not represent what really happened. Who cares? We can never know what really happened, and this version is hugely entertaining to watch.

In her 1927 novel *To the Lighthouse*, Virginia Woolf, always attuned to the importance of good food and drink at a meal, describes a dinner presided over by Mrs. Ramsey, the embodiment of the domestic spirit of conviviality and nurturing in the novel. In overseeing the meal, this character seeks a "community of feeling" in which all her friends and family, of different ages and genders, merge, at least fleetingly, into what seems akin to a living work of art, a work for which she, as hostess, is responsible: "The whole of the effort of merging and flowing and creating rest on her." It is a utopic image, and though the snippets of conversation that Woolf gives us do not reflect the perfect merger and flow that is said to result, this seems owing to the impossibility, as noted in the last chapter, of rendering in representation the vitality and warmth of good conversation as it unfurls in real time over a nice table supplied with ample food and drink.

CHAPTER 4

Bad Conversation

Just as there is a feeling of elation and goodwill that follows a good conversation, there is a feeling of irritation and sourness that follows a bad one.

Writers on the subject have enumerated what to avoid in conversation: pedantry, interruption, digression, posturing, foolishness, profanity. These "don'ts," however, can be situational. Profanity can offend with one group and create fellowship with another; interruption can sometimes denote enthusiasm; and a pontificator in one context may be a learned man in another.

Nonetheless, there are some traits that rub most everyone the wrong way: the violation of body space (a *Seinfeld* episode called this the "close talker") and the failure to listen (people only waiting to insert what they know rather than genuinely responding to what has been said).

There are also a myriad of mundane reasons for why a conversation doesn't work. One of the greatest obstacles is where it takes place. I am a great believer in coziness or what the Swedes call *hygge*. Virginia Woolf represented this at her luncheon at the men's college at Oxbridge, and the opposite of it at her dinner at the women's college. The food and drink at the latter were spare

and simple, but more detrimental was that the setting was aus-
tere and the participants uncomfortable in their second-class
status. Inevitably, as she put it, "conversation flagged."

I find it odd that many restaurants now favor industrial ma-
terials: high metal ceilings, exposed pipes and lighting fixtures,
steel tables, and chairs sometimes without backs. (My husband
will not eat in a restaurant when the chairs are uncomfortable,
a fact he can somehow assess at a glance through a window.)
Perhaps the motive behind these strenuously uncomfortable
settings is to make the clientele focus exclusively on the food,
or eat and leave as soon as possible to maximize the number of
seatings. For me, this defeats the purpose of having a meal in a
restaurant where one is freed of preparation, serving, and
cleanup, and can concentrate on talk as well as food and drink.
There are reasons why so-called traditional restaurant spaces,
with nooks and crannies, soft music, tablecloths, candles, and
discreet but impeccable service, continue to be popular, not
just with old fogies but with anyone wishing to spend a leisurely period at the table conversing. In *My Dinner with André*,
the two men eventually achieve conversational flow owing,
one feels, to the good food, the discreet service, and most of
all the warmth, comfort, and understated elegance of the restaurant in which they meet. Has anyone ever had a great, prolonged conversation at a barbecue or a picnic? Maybe, but usually such settings encourage the hasty intake of food and the
consumption of too much beer. Bloating and gas are also liable to
inhibit conversation.

In some instances, one person irritates the other. I had the
unfortunate circumstance of rubbing someone so much the
wrong way at a dinner party that that man's wife told the host
not to invite us together ever again. I was upset by the embargo,
especially because I felt that it would have been a nice challenge

to find a way back into this man's good opinion—or at least to have had a conversation with him about what annoyed him so much about me (actually, I knew what it was and would have liked to have the chance to discuss it).

A bad conversation can arise when there is a sense of inequality between the participants—when one feels the other has a superior attitude or is standing in judgment. The best conversations are equal exchanges of insight, feeling, and opinion. Even highly intellectual conversations must involve a degree of mutual openness, even vulnerability, for the participants to be safe enough to fully share what they think without feeling they might say something stupid.

Sometimes an individual simply doesn't have the capacity to have a conversation. I believe this is particularly the case with actors who have become so acclimated to reading a script that they find it hard to generate original conversation—or perhaps they become actors because they have no words of their own. In a recent Hulu series, *Only Murders in the Building*, Steve Martin plays a former television star who, when asked about his past, gives a moving account of his relationship to an abusive father that we later learn he lifted verbatim from one of his old TV scripts. In like fashion, Shakespeare's Hamlet acknowledges his incapacity to speak without a script; he laments that he can't be as expressive as the actor performing a speech about Troy's Hecuba:

> What's Hecuba to him, or he to Hecuba,
> That he should weep for her?
>   Yet I,
> A dull and muddy-mettled rascal, peak,
> Like John-a-dreams, unpregnant of my cause,
> And can say nothing.

Although we tend to think that some people are just dull, a part of me believes that, thrown together long enough, we can find points of interest in even the most unpromising individual. In my family, we often spoke about a man, the husband of one of my parents' more loquacious friends, who said nothing at the gatherings they went to until it happened that my father hit on a subject that suddenly enlivened him. The subject was M&Ms. The man worked for Mars, Inc., the candy company, and seemed to have a devotion and fascination for this product. "What was it about M&Ms that continues to appeal to the changing tastes of the American public?" my father asked. With that question, the floodgates opened, and the man responded with various theories. He and my father proceeded to have an animated discussion about M&Ms and candy in general, growing increasingly warm and joyful as they recalled the favorite candies of their youth: Sugar Babies, Red Hots, Bazooka Bubble Gum—M&Ms. Ever after, when my family was trying to get a handle on someone who seemed to us out of reach, we would ask, "What are his M&Ms?"

This supports my faith that one has only to find the key to another individual, and he or she will open to us. But then again, not always. My father reported that in subsequent encounters with Mr. M&Ms, the topic of candy having been exhausted, the man lapsed back into his usual silent mode. In other words, some people have nothing to say beyond their M&Ms.

Sometimes the issue is not dullness but incompatibility—of diametrically opposed tastes that link to larger issues of identity and politics. The famous meeting that took place in 1922 between James Joyce and Marcel Proust is a case in point. Both men were, by this time, on the way to becoming celebrated writers, giants of literary modernism, but their styles and personali-

ties could not have been more different. There are many scenarios reported about their meeting, but in none do the two
men get along. Here are two amusing examples:

> PROUST: I have never read your works, Mr. Joyce.
> JOYCE: I have never read your works, Mr. Proust.

And:

> PROUST: Ah, Monsieur Joyce, you know the Princess . . .
> JOYCE: No, Monsieur.
> PROUST: then you know Madame . . .
> JOYCE: No, Monsieur.

The gulf between them was later summarized by Joyce as follows: "Proust would talk only of duchesses, while I was more
concerned with chambermaids." In other words, class interests
that carried over into esthetic taste irreparably divided these
two great writers.

It's interesting to think how what, for one person, would be
entirely alienating and even traumatic, for another is relatively
benign. I have never forgotten the passage in Mary Catherine
Bateson's *With a Daughter's Eye*, a biography of her parents, an-
thropologists Margaret Mead and Gregory Bateson, in which she
describes a conversation with her father while they were doing
fieldwork together in Switzerland: "My father looked at me rather
meditatively one day and said, he supposed . . . that really the
only reason we shouldn't go to bed together . . . was the danger
of genetic damage if I should get pregnant? And I said, equally
low-keyed, that I thought there were other reasons too. The question was such a mild one that we could continue the conversation
about culs-de-sac in the evolutionary process with only momen-
tary tension." Here's a case where the family lexicon was such that
a blatantly inappropriate remark, presented in anthropological

terms, could be assimilated into conversation. Mary Catherine knew, from an early age, that her father was a brilliant kook, and she took such comments in her stride.

The issue of ideology as it inhibits conversation has come to the fore recently within the walls of academia. The university used to be referred to as an ivory tower, reflecting its pursuit of disinterested knowledge and its aloofness from worldly concerns; it was supposed to be a safe space for wide-ranging, uninhibited conversation. But what once seemed an unassailable truth has since been called into question.

The problem is that "safety" can have different meanings, depending upon one's perspective. One kind of safety protects free speech, another protects against statements that might offend or pain the listener. In both cases, there is a risk of extremism. Free speech can devolve into hate speech. Protecting against hurt can become so broad and subjective as to make most anything that doesn't tow a certain broad definition of niceness to be out of bounds. The question becomes: when does free speech become hate speech, and when does the designation of hate speech become so elastic as to be meaningless?

One thing is certain: it is hard to have a conversation with a true believer. If you disagree with a Marxist, he will tell you that you are hopelessly trapped inside a corrupt capitalistic system. If you disagree with a classical Freudian, she will label your denial a sign of repression. A religious zealot will say you are at best a lost soul, at worst possessed by the devil. This kind of thinking has emerged recently around the concept of social justice. Because this is such a morally charged idea, someone who disagrees with the consensus view can be seen as not just wrong but bad. Sometimes, I am at a meeting or listening to a panel and am overwhelmed by the self-congratulatory "virtue signaling" going on around me: everyone is determined to register as virtuous according to what the arbiters of virtue have established this to be.

I have also been in situations where everyone seems to agree on a given matter, but when I look at the faces of people who have not spoken, I see that they look unhappy. I suspect that they don't agree but don't want to risk giving their opinion for fear of hurting others' feelings or being ostracized as bad people. It takes a certain amount of practice as well as courage to articulately counter a prevailing point of view.

Groupthink refers to a tendency for people in groups to share the same values to a point that can be inhibiting of individual will and creativity. *Grouptalk* is the corollary to this or, rather, the form of its conditioning and reinforcement. The sense of comfort and nurturance that a group can engender can also create an atmosphere where it is hard to diverge from the consensus opinion. In a group that adheres to a rigid set of principles, to deviate or even question any of these principles can seem like an act of violation. The individual can suffer— or fear to suffer—ridicule, punishment, or ostracism. Instances of this occurred during the 1950s when no one dared to speak up against the ideological bully, Joseph McCarthy. It also happened in reverse. African American writer Richard Wright describes the climate of a Communist Party meeting in the 1930s when he opposed a party edict: "I saw that even those who agreed with me would not support me. . . . When a man was informed of the wish of the party he submitted, even though he knew with all the strength of his brain that the wish was not a wise one, was one that would ultimately harm the party's interests." A book like George Orwell's *Nineteen Eighty-Four* dramatizes the predicament. It has been assigned forever in high schools and should serve as a cautionary tale for even the most unreflective young mind if presented with vigor by a teacher; unfortunately, I suspect its longevity in the curriculum has made it stale, and it is now taught and, therefore, read by rote.

By the same token, our current awareness of how those in positions of power can manipulate and coerce us is more developed than it once was. People used to take the word of their politicians, their bosses, their religious leaders, and their media commentators as gospel. Dating probably from the Viet Nam War when the public learned that their governing officials had lied to them, skepticism about the sincerity and truth of these authorities began to take hold and has increased with the advent of new sources of information—and misinformation—via the internet. We are thrown back on our own resources to determine what is true, and this makes conversation with others that much more important, but also more difficult. We need to listen and test our ideas against what others think, without necessarily casting judgment or engaging in violent argument. This can be hard to do when we believe we are right. But we would do well to recall Montaigne's famous phrase: *Que sais-je?* (What do I know?).

The relationship between training talk and coercive talk is another area worth considering. An organization like Alcoholics Anonymous has as its goal the treatment of individuals who have almost destroyed themselves through their dependence on alcohol. A church youth group may want to help young people bond with each other and learn values, professed by the religion, that will help them navigate the pitfalls of adolescence. A corporation may want to help its managers be more sensitive to individuals who have traditionally been discriminated against. Yet the line between helping people form good habits and indoctrinating them into a prescribed set of beliefs can be a fine one. Indeed, the problem arises because the group ethos can be so comforting and necessary to an individual's well-being that opposing it feels frightening or impossible.

The nature of a group seems to me to be established from its beginnings so that when people say they are surprised when they find that people they thought were open and flexible are actually dogmatic and intolerant, I am skeptical. A group that is open to dissent will reveal that openness immediately, while one that is not will soon show that it holds to certain hard assumptions that cannot be questioned. For example, everyone in the group assumes you go to church or support abortion or have the money to vacation in the south of France (these examples fall into the categories of religion, politics, and class that are common targets for grouptalk). The initial premise may seem benign enough (or one that you happen to agree with), but by being an assumption that cannot brook opposition, it tends to give rise to subsidiary premises, so that the group becomes associated with a network of beliefs very hard to argue with or oppose. People in the group not only may fail to understand someone not sharing their opinion but can see a disagreement as a threat and the individual who disagrees as a bad or dangerous person.

Grouptalk is different from groupthink in that it need not mean that everyone in the group shares the same ideas. I am convinced that even when all the people present have more or less the same position on something, when the atmosphere is one of grouptalk, the feeling is uneasy. There is an implicit sense that some part of oneself has been silenced or truncated. This is bad conversation; everyone knows it, though no one may be willing to admit it.

The opposite of grouptalk is argument—not the sort of gentle argument that fuels conversation by supporting difference, but argument in which parties are vehemently and self-righteously divided. "I never yet saw an instance of one of two disputants convincing the other by argument," wrote Thomas Jefferson to his grandson. "I have seen many of them getting warm, becoming rude, & shooting one another." Yet again and again, I see people espouse their positions so unequivocally that the other side is prompted to do the same. The conversation quickly escalates into what anthropologist Gregory Bateson called *schismogenesis*: an intensification of opposition between two parties. Bateson used the example of the Cold War: without controls on nuclear armaments and related diplomatic safeguards, the United States and the Soviet Union would have destroyed each other. Similarly, a determination to hold unwaveringly to a viewpoint that someone else opposes is likely to blow up a conversation and, beyond that, a friendship. (Fortunately, we are beyond the era of the duel—but, as Jefferson notes, one can easily see how this kind of argument could result in a shooting.)

Our society abounds in bad conversation. It is modeled for us on television by politicians and pundits. We see it in the shouting matches captured on YouTube. Bad conversation can be entertaining, even as it foments ill will and division. Good conversation, on the other hand, is less frequently modeled, mostly because it is rare and less fun to watch than to engage in. The best training for it is the college seminar, which I will discuss in chapter 9.

CHAPTER 5

Talking with the French

I spent the year after I graduated from college as an *assistante* in a high school in Lille, a city in the north of France not far from the Belgian border. At the time, Lille was a rather depressed and shabby city (it has since grown more glamorous and commercially vibrant). When I told Parisians that I was living in Lille, they invariably shook their heads and murmured with that mix of pity and contempt particular to the citizens of that city: "c'est triste."

Yet Lille, if it was not Paris, was still France, and it had the advantage over the capital in having practically no American residents at the time. Hence, I had a pure experience of French life during a formative period in my development: I became exposed to conversation with French people, who I believe talk better than anyone else.

I am aware that I am idealizing the French. I also know that my ideas about them derive from a time long ago (forty years!), and that whenever I returned to visit, I was not there long enough to amend that early impression. Once we make assumptions about something, we tend to reinforce them, whether they continue to be true or not. This has its positive and its negative aspects. If we love something, we continue to

love it. If our initial feelings are negative, we find them reinforced. The latter, we should work against. The former, I am
content to leave alone.

Those of us who came into contact with things French in
our youth tend to retain an unflagging affection for them. I
believe this is because these things have been introduced to us
in the context of French conversation. There is a quality to that
talk that appeals to the adolescent imagination. Certainly, the
French people, if I can generalize, have peccadillos and prejudices that deserve criticism, which I will address later, but
there is no denying that they love conversation and are extraor-
dinarily good at it. I would borrow from Ernest Hemingway's
statement, the final phrase becoming the title of his memoir:
"If you are lucky enough to have lived in Paris as a young man,
then wherever you go for the rest of your life, it stays with you,
for Paris is a moveable feast." Expanding the gender and the
place to include women and other regions of France, this statement certainly applies to me, and I think continues to hold
true for others today.

It helps, of course, that French is among the most mellifluous
of languages and the most subtly and delightfully expressive. I
love the way the French can draw out an idea through the twists
and turns of words or condense it smartly with a few, clipped
ones. I love certain words in French that serve as transitions or
fillers: *donc, bref, eh bien, finalement, apparement*—these words
carry a kind of frilly authority, a teasing mix of the masculine
and feminine. It's true that certain locutions have a way of seeming more clever and profound in French than they would be in
English—but that is the allure of the language; it carries its intelligence in its tonality, cadence, and structure and allows one
to feel oneself to be smarter than one would otherwise be,
which in itself is an incitement to be smarter.

The French can be world-weary and cynical but not despair-
ing or depressive—a fine balance that they can maintain
because of the stylish nature of how they use words. Take, for
example, the aphorisms of François de la Rochefoucauld, who
in the seventeenth century created a compendium of indict-
ments of the hypocrisy of human beings in society without
himself abandoning that society. Here are a few of his *Maxims*
plucked out at random:

> #19: We all have strength to bear our neighbor's burden.
> #31: Had we no faults, we should not take such pleasure in
> discovering them in others.
> #39: Egotism plays many parts, even that of altruism.
> #62: Sincerity is open-heartedness. Few people have it; in
> most cases it is a delicate dissimulation practiced to gain
> the confidence of others.
> #93: Old people like to give good advice, since they can no
> longer set bad examples.

One feels the jolt of recognition reading these aphorisms. Is this
cynicism or realism? It's hard to say; only that it is somehow
French and lends itself to conversation.

If La Rochefoucauld incites conversation with his pithy aphorisms, Michel de Montaigne, writing a century earlier, pioneered the most conversational of literary forms, the meandering personal essay. Montaigne's essays are both analytical and
self-revealing; they treat the reader as an intimate who he assumes is interested in the minutiae of the author's intellectual
ruminations and his mundane daily life. Indeed, these are the
ingredients of good conversation. Montaigne's *Que sais-je?* is
also a reminder of the limitations within which we operate,
what we ought to tell ourselves whenever we feel too certain we
are right and are digging in our heels during a conversation.

It has been suggested that Montaigne's *Essays* were prompted by the death of his friend, Étienne de la Boétie, to whom one of the longest pieces, "Of Friendship," is dedicated. Montaigne admits to having suffered greatly the loss of that friendship, which seems to have been grounded in lively, wide-ranging conversation. The essays can be seen as Montaigne's attempt to continue the conversation with his friend in his imagination and transfer it to the page.

Montaigne's most famous essay, "Of Cannibals," is a wonderfully original discussion of the customs and mores of different peoples—an insightful understanding of how we tend to label others as primitive and not see the brutality of our own culture. Shakespeare is said to have been influenced by this essay in creating the character of Caliban in *The Tempest*, the creature native to the island who delivers a scathing critique of his master, Prospero, the embodiment of Western patriarchal culture: "You taught me language and my profit on't / Is I know how to curse." The statement encapsulates the danger of language when it develops outside of the reciprocity and mutual respect that comes from "equal" conversation.

Speaking French as a nonnative during the year I spent in France allowed me to understand the dynamics of conversation more fully. It also helped me know myself better than I would otherwise have done. Loving the French language as I do, I am inclined to see it as uniquely suited to self-reflection and reinvention—and perhaps, relatedly, to distancing myself from myself and hence relinquishing responsibility for my own words in a unique way. In Thomas Mann's *Magic Mountain*, the hero, Hans Castorp, lapses from his native German into French when he finally becomes intimate with Clavdia Chauchat, the woman he has been obsessed with from afar: "parler français, c'est parler sans parler, en quelque manière—sans responsabilité, ou comme nous parlons en rêve," he explains to Clavdia ("speaking in French is to speak without speaking, in a sense—without responsibility, or as we would speak in a dream"). Mann, in the afterword to the novel, further explains Castorp's use of French: "It eases his embarrassment and helps him to say things he could never have dared say in his own language."

This French interlude in *Magic Mountain* (which, not knowing German, I otherwise read in translation) reinforced my romantic sense of the language. Yet to be fair, I know that any foreign language, if you become moderately good at it, can be liberating and exciting in this way. It can allow you to lose yourself and, simultaneously, become more aware of how you interact with others—to more consciously shape the self you present to the world. I realize that not everyone has the opportunity or facility to learn another language well enough to experience what I am describing. But I suspect that a similar experience can be obtained by spending time in a country where one's native language is spoken in a very different cultural context (Jamaica, Ireland, or Kenya, for example). On consideration, even another part of the country will do (our daughter spent time teaching high school in southern Arkansas, and her stay there was like visiting another country with its own customs and phrases: deer hunting on the weekends and "y'all" in every other sentence, not to mention "yes, ma'am" and "yes, sir" in addressing one's elders; she relished operating in that lexicon much the way I relished speaking French).

Still, there are things about French culture that make it uniquely conducive to conversation and its corollary, self-knowledge, and I am thankful that, having had access to only one foreign language, French was the one I learned. This was not coincidental. My mother was a high school French teacher. Her interest was in everything French, but she concentrated most on perfecting her ability to speak the language. She was continually brushing up on her idioms and updating her slang. She prided herself on impeccable grammar, never omitting a subjective or mistaking the gender of a noun or the form of a past participle. She loved the fact that, when she went to France, she was often mistaken for a French woman (though generally from a different region of the country than the one in which she found herself).

Since I adored my mother, I sought to imitate her and embrace her enthusiasms, though, oddly, I never was able to speak French half as well as she did. This was partially because I lacked a so-called "ear" for language, and partially because of a failure to work at getting better at it. In retrospect, I see that it suited me to speak well enough but not too well. Perhaps I wished not to compete with my adored mother in this arena. Perhaps I realized that I would never be quite good enough and that being unabashedly faulty allowed me to be consigned to the status of an American who tries her best, a position that allows for the *noblesse oblige* that the French enjoy.

Whatever the reason, my flawed French served me well, for I am convinced that there is an existential value in not being entirely fluent in a second language. It allows you to hover both inside and outside that language and thereby view the experience more deliberately and self-consciously. I'm sure there is a degree of rationalization to this viewpoint, but I hold to it and will trot it out whenever I encounter foreign students at my university who are struggling with their English: "Enjoy your position between two cultures," I tell them. "If you stay in this country long enough, you will become fluent, but that will be both a gain and a loss, since you will no longer have the same kind of double perspective on things."

I have spoken about the French language as uniquely conducive to conversation. What is it about French culture and history that accounts for this? I explain this by invoking the nation's most influential philosopher, René Descartes. The "Cartesian method"—the form of inquiry pioneered by Descartes— conceives of *thought* as the highest of all values, and enshrines self-consciousness and doubt as the means of testing and interrogating thought. This testing and interrogation are the basis for conversation, which never stays pat or finds closure.

Descartes's famous dictum was "cogito, ergo sum": "I think, therefore I am." I have considered how differently the result would be if the logic were reversed. Not "I think, therefore I am," but "I am, therefore I think." The latter would see thought emerging spontaneously and naturally out of existence rather than being the guarantor of existence. "I am, therefore I think" leaves one without the responsibility for self-making that "I think, therefore I am" requires. (One can see how Descartes's statement connects to the French philosophy of Existentialism, which requires one to both acknowledge the absurdity of life and take responsibility for making it meaningful.) The American way, one might argue, is to act first and rationalize (think about it) later ("I am, therefore I think").

In the Cartesian lexicon, which I equate with the logic of French culture, thought takes precedence over (or is the surrogate for) action. The introduction of French theory into American academia five decades ago can be said to have paved the way for a new kind of activism that we are seeing today in progressive bastions across the country—an activism that centers on language rather than literal action.

I would also suggest that there is an interesting distinction to be drawn between thought and imagination that separates the

French from the English, and that connects to conversation. In English literature there is a huge premium placed on the imagination. This goes back to the Elizabethan period where Shakespeare often asks his audience to use their imagination to supply what is missing or can't be represented on stage. In the prologue to *Henry V*, for example, he has the Chorus entreat us to imagine an army in one man: "Piece out our imperfections with your thoughts / Into a thousand parts divide one man, / And make imaginary puissance." The call to the imagination is also a hallmark of the English Romantic poets for whom the natural world supplied the groundwork, and the individual imagination supplied the spark to give it form and meaning. In "Lines Written a Few Miles from Tintern Abbey," William Wordsworth expounds on "all the mighty world / Of eye, and ear,—both what they half create, / And what perceive." And in Book VI of his epic poem, *The Prelude, or Growth of a Poet's Mind*, he invokes the imagination directly:

> Imagination—here the Power so called.
> Through sad incompetence of human speech,
> That awful Power rose from the mind's abyss
> Like an unfathered vapour that enwraps,
> At once, some lonely traveller.

For Wordsworth, imagination, "higher reason," transcends the "sad incompetence of human speech" and nourishes the solitary soul.

Thought, by contrast, is better explored with someone else— shared and amplified through conversation. The French facilitate thought by having a centralized educational system with a curriculum that is lockstep through to high school graduation. Its nationwide test for college entry, the baccalaureate, means that those who go on to college have achieved a shared competence across disciplines: everyone can discourse together on a group of works that they have been conditioned to find great and to parse according to a standardized method.

This accounts for the seemingly high level of intellectualism on the part of the French people: everyone knows the same books and can talk about them in the same, elevated way. I will never forget my first trip to the country, taking a taxi to my hotel and having the driver explain the history of the city and then segue into a discussion of the character of Rastignac in Balzac's *Père Goriot* and his travails in the Paris of the mid-nineteenth century, which he then connected to certain upwardly mobile elements in the society of the present (there is always a markedly leftist turn to the French educational system). It was an amazing piece of literary and sociological discourse. This would be like having a taxi driver in New York City suddenly start expounding on the tribulations of Jay Gatsby as they related to contemporary life. I would have thought that that taxi conversation was a singular event had I not had a subsequent conversation with a taxi driver some years later about another nineteenth-century French novel, Stendhal's *The Red and the Black*. In this case, the driver assumed I was interested in his opinion about the hero, Julien Sorel's passion for Madame de Renal. As it happens, I was—and we proceeded to have a lively discussion about the ethics of adultery, which, in stereotypical French fashion, he appeared to find perfectly natural, expressed with a shrug and one of the most commonly used of French phrases: *c'est normal*. (Roger Cohen, in a *New York Times* article about his own infatuation with France, amended this to *bof, c'est normal*— *bof* being an untranslatable French verbal shrug.)

More than a decade ago, when Nicolas Sarkozy was president of France (denigrated at the time as an American-style anti-intellectual), he had the temerity to criticize the seventeenth-century French novel *La Princesse de Clèves* by the revered writer and salonnière Madame de La Fayette. The book has been a staple in the French high school curriculum since time immemorial. It is an esoteric work—a delicate set piece, detailing the minutiae of life in the court of Louis XIV and the attenuated sentiments that flourished within it. It is unimaginable that an American high school student could be made to read such a book. And yet Sarkozy's denigration of *La Princesse de Clèves* met with a storm of outrage in France from people of all ages and social classes, with rallies being staged on behalf of the novel and vicious attacks on Sarkozy as a worthless philistine. The fact is that most French, whatever their social class or background, have a deep respect for the literary tradition that was pummeled into them at school and, with it, a deep respect for the intellect and for ideas. They are comfortable thinking abstractly, and abstract thought is the motor for good conversation.

The French often begin a conversation with a conventional, even clichéd point. In some ways, they are a very conformist people, which, given the conformity of their education, makes sense. Even in their fashion, for which they are known, the look is uniform, with no outlandish styles or bright colors. When my husband wore a red sweater on the streets of Paris on one occasion, there were stares; he might have been naked from the waist up.

But one could also say that French conformism and conventionality are a base, like the stock used for a good soup, from which one can proceed to create something new and delectable. Thus, in broaching a favorite subject like the difference between themselves and other nationalities, they will begin with the predictable edict that the Germans are correct, the British are cold, and the Americans are impetuous. From here they can proceed to expand. They tend to think in binaries, as British Mauritian historian Sudhir Hazareesingh has noted: "openings and closures, stasis and transformation, freedom and determinism, unity and diversity, civilization and barbarity, and progress and decadence." Yet these divisions are never static (even when stasis is one of them)—always subject to rumination, elaboration, and revision, if not outright reversal. If, in one part of the conversation, they have dubbed Americans as cowboys and hotheads, not thinking about the repercussions of our actions, in another they will shift and make us Puritans, stuck in stodgy, cautious behavior. If the contradiction is pointed out, they may elaborate by clarifying the contexts involved and finding a bridge between these seeming opposites. At some point, faced with a more stubborn sort of contradiction, they may simply shrug indifferently and conclude *c'est normal*—the end point of any mistake or failure. The last refuge of French conversation lies in the shrugging acknowledgment that whatever is odd, contradictory, or mistaken is perfectly normal. There is a kind of Whitmanesque aspect to this: "Do I contradict myself? Very well then I contradict myself." (But given the conformity and, until recently, the relative homogeneity of the population, they might recoil from the second part of Whitman's statement: "I am large, I contain multitudes.")

My time in France, despite the occasional foray into the classroom to be tittered at for my American wardrobe by a group of ultra-chic French schoolgirls (my job, by the way, stipulated that I teach, not English, but American), was mostly devoted to conversing. I am amazed by the amount of time I spent in cafés sipping martinis (not the English kind favored by James

Bond; the French kind, which refers to the brand name of sweet vermouth, served straight) and discussing "the abyss."

The French elevation of conversation as a major cultural pastime can be traced back to the rise of the literary salon in the seventeenth century. This period in French life has been called the Age of Conversation because it placed a value on the assemblage and orchestration of talk among a diverse, but carefully chosen, group of people. The great salonnières were intelligent, often self-educated women who were enormously tasteful, verbally adept, and charming. They had mastered the art of conversation at a high level and attracted interesting people to their home at prescribed hours, weekly and sometimes daily.

The Marquise de Rambouillet is often labeled the first of the great salonnières (the term not coined, however, until the nineteenth century). She developed her coterie toward the beginning of the seventeenth century and was supportive of talent and productivity among her favorites. She was instrumental in clarifying the work of the newly founded Académie Française in its attempts to standardize the French language. Her salon has been seen as a proto-feminist site, as she welcomed women as well as men and encouraged female literary production. Madame de La Fayette wrote *La Princesse de Clèves* under her auspices. She and her friends were satirized by Molière in his 1659 play, *Les Précieuses Ridicules* (*précieuses* were posturing, erudite women who a century later in England would be called "bluestockings"). Unfortunately, Nicolas Sarkozy did not have Molière's satirical gift, no less his ability to express himself in rhyming couplets when he took aim at Madame de La Fayette's novel.

The court of Louis XIV attempted to close down the salons as an impingement on its own elite circle, which was also overseen by women—notably Louis's mistress, Madame de Pompadour and, later, the mistress of his son, Louis XV, Madame du Barry. Nonetheless, the independent salons continued and are said to have helped foment the French Revolution by being a gathering place for the *philosophes*, male political thinkers Voltaire, Diderot, D'Alembert, and others.

The Marquise de Lambert is often cited as the bridge between the seventeenth- and eighteenth-century salonnières. She extended the link to the Académie Française that the Marquise de Rambouillet had established, and produced her own writing on the subject of education. Her wide-ranging interests attracted scientists as well as literary figures. Later, the Marquise de Deffand entertained many of the luminaries of the Enlightenment until a rival salon emerged under the younger Madame de Lespinasse. Deffand had taken Lespinasse under her wing, but the girl's popularity turned her into a rival and resulted in a spectacular falling out, with followers obliged to take sides as one would in the case of divorced spouses.

Another salonnière, Madame Geoffrin, is generally seen as leading the major Enlightenment salon, hosting the philosophes, and providing funds for the famed *Encyclopédie*. The influence of the salon can be seen in some of Denis Diderot's work, which presents ideas in the form of dialogues between Diderot (or a fictional interlocutor) and another personage.

A later salonnière, Madame Roland, the most famous of the period leading into the French Revolution, encouraged her followers to study documents like the Declaration of Independence and cultivate radical views. After the revolution got under way, owing to her alliance with the Girondin politicians then out of favor, she was arrested and executed by that cruel symbol of French revolutionary justice, the guillotine. It is ironic to think that the salons, which were built on the concept of a certain kind

of indulgent leisure, would give rise to one of the bloodiest of all
revolutions—but then irony is very French.

The personalities and melodramatic scenarios associated
with the salonnières whom I have mentioned—and others that
I have not—are taught to every French schoolchild, reflecting
how important these women and their gatherings were in the
country's intellectual and cultural history.

Salons continued into the nineteenth century. Among the
most famous in literature is the one Marcel Proust describes in
his multivolume novel about nineteenth fin de siècle society,
A La Recherche du Temps Perdu: that of Madame Verdurin, a
society hostess modeled on Leontine Lippmann, better known
by her married name Madame Arman de Caillavet (a Jew by
birth, she was characterized by Proust as a Christian and an
anti-Semite). Throughout the novel's seven books, the character of Marcel, a loose surrogate for the author, makes numerous visits to the salon of Madame Verdurin. She is a member
of the bourgeoisie, excluded from the gatherings of the aristocracy (a recapitulation, one could say, of Marquise de Rambouillet's salon with respect to the court of Louis XIV). She
pretends not to care about class distinctions and puts forward
her acolytes as superior because of their ties to art and culture.
Her "petit clan" includes a noted novelist, composer, painter,
and academic alongside a few minor aristocrats and courtesans. They meet regularly at her home in Paris or in the country and are expected to be loyal in exchange for a comfortable
setting, lavish food and drink, an occasional musical performance, and continual conversation.

Proust, a consummate snob himself, clearly intends us to have
contempt for Madame Verdurin, yet he also makes clear the shallowness and bigotry of the aristocratic gatherings that snub her
and her little clan. In the last chapter, the novel shifts to a later

time, after the First World War, when things have changed considerably. Marcel, having been long isolated from society, now returns to attend a party given by some of his old friends. He sees that Madame Verdurin has achieved her secret aspiration and been incorporated into the aristocracy through a second marriage to the highest pedigreed of individuals, the Prince of Guermantes, transforming her into the new Princess of Guermantes. She now is central to the group that had once excluded her. With the end of the Great War and society reconstituted, this group has become much like the bourgeois salon that the aristocrats formerly scorned. Everyone blithely ignores this irony and carries on under the assumption that *c'est normal*.

According to the philosopher Jürgen Habermas, salon culture, so inherent a part of French history, helped by newspapers and other forms of communication, laid the groundwork for the "public sphere," where the spectacle of the state was replaced by the dialogue of the public, as epitomized in the French Revolution.

The salon also laid the cultural groundwork for the café culture with which France continues to be associated. Although cafés existed in France dating from the seventeenth century (and coffee houses in England from the same period), these were more male precincts than what we know today as the lively site for social interaction between the sexes and among diverse peoples.

One can explain the shift by the fact that Paris underwent dramatic renovation under the direction of the architect Baron Georges Haussmann in the middle of the nineteenth century, creating the wide, chestnut-tree-lined boulevards we know today. The numerous small restaurants with outside dining that sprang up in this wonderfully designed space supplied its guests with a perch from which to view the variety of human life as it passed. It also allowed patrons to take a coffee or a snack at any time of day. There were so many cafés with so much seating that people could sit for hours without being expected to move on. Hence, the City of Light became the City of Conversation.

I could argue on behalf of afternoon tea in Britain as encouraging of conversation, and I will discuss the once-flourishing British gentlemen's clubs as enclaves for gender-segregated conversation in a subsequent chapter. I know that there has long existed a vibrant coffee culture in Turkey, Cuba, Mexico, Italy, Israel, and many Arab nations. But for reasons that may not be defensible, it is the French whom I associate most dramatically with conversation as I know and love it. Hence my ideal afternoon: sitting with a friend in a café in the fifth arrondissement (the so-called Latin Quarter), in sight of the Sorbonne, on a balmy spring day, conversing in desultory fashion over an expresso and a *pain chocolat* about such topics as the nature of love, the relativity of beauty, and the likelihood of life after death, before returning home to dress for dinner at a little bistro, equally conducive to conversation.

The French love of ideas captivated me during my year abroad and fed my lifelong addiction to conversation. I continually bump into people who have had a similar experience and who, upon retirement, make a beeline for the Alliance Française in their city to brush up on their French in the hope of purchasing a *pied à terre* in Paris (some people I know have actually done this).

Yet seductive and charming as French conversation can be, it is not without its limitations. Certain topics are off-limits for the French. Not sex, of course—it is entirely permissible to talk and insinuate on this subject (though perhaps less so in recent years). But anything to do with money and with careerist aspirations is deeply frowned on—perhaps because it goes against the grain of the desultory, non-goal-oriented nature of conversation as a pastime. It may also be the result of conditioning that goes back to the French Revolution, a violent upheaval that no other Western European country experienced to the same degree. Indeed, not the Revolution itself but the Reign of Terror that occurred from 1793 to 1794 seems to me to be at the root of a certain kind of French reticence. Better not to reveal too much or put oneself forward in too great a fashion or one's head may be metaphorically if not literally chopped off. One is reminded of that fearsome contraption every time one walks through the Place de la Concorde, where the royal family, including the lovely Marie Antoinette, lost their heads in front of an enthusiastic crowd. The historical memory of such events would certainly have impressed itself into the French psyche in such a way as to instigate a certain kind of reflexive circumlocution—a determination not to reveal oneself that contributes to the indeterminacy and mystification that makes French conversation interesting and keeps it going.

I recall one gathering where I was taken by a friend during my time in France. There was a great deal of talk, but no one asked me a single question; it was as though I was invisible. I eventually learned that I was supposed to casually insert myself into the conversation, become, as it were, a part of the intellectual whole before I could become known as an individual. This is a difficult and daunting kind of initiation, one that is bound to exclude people who cannot hold their own. But then, French culture is intellectually snobbish and exclusionary, a by-product, one could say, of its drive to discriminate, which extends to people as well as ideas. Americans are far more open and curious about the practical lives (rather than the intellectual lives) of others. What we tend to not be able to do is keep an idea going rather than simply hacking at it in perfunctory fashion before moving on to another topic. "Get to the point," an American might say, or "What are you driving at?" Impatience is an American attribute; the French take more pleasure in the journey than the destination. They've had practice sitting in cafés, stirring their tiny expressos, smoking their cigarettes, and letting an idea unfurl at its own pace.

Smoking, that is, until recently. The country has finally gotten the message about cigarettes. This recognition is not universal, mind you, and you will still see people sucking on their Gauloises or Gitanes (or, if seeking a more cosmopolitan look, Marlboros). But what used to be as prevalent as a baguette under the arm has become far less common as French people seem to have finally acknowledged the dangers of smoking. This is a good thing for the nation's health, but possibly a detriment to café society. After all, to smoke a cigarette—extract it from a squashed packet in one's breast pocket or pocketbook, search for a match, light up and puff—has long been the accepted punctuation for French talk, a way of segueing from one idea to another, of passing over an awkward moment, or simply giving the impression that one is contemplating some deep issue. I began smoking during my year in France and had to quit once I returned to health-conscious America. This actually wasn't very hard since the need for the cigarette as the adjunct to conversation wasn't part of the American conversational ritual. Indeed, there was no American conversational ritual, and it took some time before I found anyone who could engage in the kind of talk that I found in France with most everyone, including the concierge who tended the building where I lived. She seemed to lead an otherwise threadbare existence with her cats but nonetheless had a lot to say about La Fontaine.

The French are willing to extrapolate on an idea even if it is impractical or outright wrong. They are at home with the necessary disconnect that exists between theory and practice. What Americans might call hypocrisy, the French simply see as playful theorizing, not to be taken too seriously. The French have long had a tradition, for example, of supporting left-leaning ideas while being happily ensconced in a bourgeois lifestyle that includes the finest food and wine. One of the interesting hallmarks of the French (especially Parisians) is to have a somewhat shabby exterior to their homes and a luxe and manicured interior. Is this another by-product of that long ago revolution? Don't advertise your wealth? French people like to intone the aphorism of having "leur coeurs à gauche et leur portefeuilles à droite" (their hearts on the left but their wallets on the right). How many times have I heard this recited to me by someone in a well-tailored suit who, after stating it, continues his rousing advocacy of the work of Frantz Fanon, the revolutionary theorist of the underclass.

American life has begun to mimic some aspects of French café culture with the ubiquity of Starbucks franchises and a myriad of independent coffee shops that have proliferated in our cities. These do not have the cultural history of the French café or tabac (the latter so-called because they sell cigarettes), but they are making inroads. Among young people, in particular, the coffee shop, prior to the COVID-19 pandemic, had become a standard work space, and I see it becoming only more so as we return to more normal but flexible work schedules. Walk into any neighborhood coffee shop and you will see a line of young people seated at small tables with their laptops open, working away. Since COVID-19 has also forced people around the world to locate their restaurants outside, I wonder if this will make other national populations more like the French.

And yet, even as we mimic the form of the French café, we are hard-pressed to imitate its substance. For the French are experts at not working—or rather, at delegating work to one part of their lives and then embarking on leisure, mostly in the form of conversation (though also sex) in the other. American students in cafés are working at their computers and rarely talking together. Yet by planting themselves in such spots, I suspect that what they really want to do is talk, if only they could find the way to do it—to puncture the invisible barrier that divides each table from the one beside it, each computer screen from its neighbor's. The desire to hang out in the coffee shop rather than in one's apartment or the library reflects an implicit, perhaps inchoate desire to connect in conversation, even if it isn't happening. Maybe, post-COVID-19, our defenses down and our isolation more bothersome, it will.

CHAPTER 6

Schools of Talk

History is dotted with stories of people who found solace, love, friendship, inspiration, and political support through ongoing interaction with each other. We know some of the content of those relationships from their epistolary correspondence, since writing can be preserved and read by posterity. The loss of letter writing, owing to the internet, is sure to truncate our record of human relationships.

Famous correspondents like Thomas Jefferson and John Adams, Zora Neale Hurston and Franz Boas, Jean-Paul Sartre and Simone de Beauvoir, Elizabeth Bishop and Robert Lowell, and Hannah Arendt and Martin Heidegger come to mind and offer the student of history and culture important material for understanding these august individuals' life and work. In some instances, the entire relationship existed on paper and that, to me, says something about the degree of control that they were able to—and perhaps needed to—maintain. In other instances, there were more than letters that linked these people; they spent time together engaging in conversation, sometimes supplemented by physical intimacy.

When a relationship is both a living one and a literary one, I am prompted to ask: are the letters the mere residue, the frozen tokens of something far more vital and elusive? I tend to think so. If sexual intimacy is involved that adds another element of mystery to the relationship—a topic for another day. But what makes conversation, like sex, so retrospectively poignant is that it exists in a particular moment and then is gone. If we think of conversation as an art, then it is more like food and theater than it is like poetry and film, though in fact it is like neither in that even a meal and a theatrical production have a blueprint, whereas a conversation happens spontaneously—it is an improvisational art form. We can return to our friend and talk more, but that last conversation is a unique thing, consigned to the past, never to be retrieved. And of course, when our friend dies, the next conversation can never happen. (I write this having lost two of my most cherished conversational partners within the past several years and feel deprived every day of the unique quality and vitality of their talk.)

Cultural history has enshrined certain groups of people who met regularly and conversed together. We know about such conversations because records were kept by some of the participants or by onlookers, and because the groups in question have gone on to contribute important work to society.

I want to briefly describe a number of these groups and organize them under specific categories. This will allow me to discuss different kinds of conversation without trying to be comprehensive. At the same time, I realize that what I am doing is mildly absurd. The groups that I discuss overlap and hold only loosely to the categories that I have assigned them.

I have also confined myself to England, America, and France, owing to the limitations of my education and knowledge, although I know that there have been important groups associated with other nations. I also know that in some of the cases that I describe the interactions were not conversations in the best sense of the term. Indeed, they may have been negative examples of what good conversations should be like—not having been present, it is hard to pass judgment (though I sometimes will). Mostly what I can say is that these groups are famous as gatherings or movements, which in itself may reflect a limitation inherent in the way they conversed. James Baldwin wrote astutely on this point in his essay, "Down at the Cross: Letter from a Region in My Mind," from *The Fire Next Time*: "People always seem to band together in accordance to a principle that has nothing to do with love, a principle that releases them from personal responsibility." Since I have associated love and personal responsibility with good conversation, Baldwin's point seems cautionary. And yet I believe that these groups do offer some insight into conversation. Their prominence serves to illuminate the kinds of issues that were being discussed in various corners of the culture that they both reflected and helped to shape.

Let me reiterate the point I have made earlier in this book that any generalized statement about conversation where we are not present is liable to be inadequate or wrong. Dr. Johnson, presumed to be the consummate conversationist, is quoted as saying that "the happiest conversation [is] where there is no competition, no vanity, but a calm quiet interchange of sentiments." Yet he himself was competitive and vain, and not the least bit calm and quiet in his manner of conversing. Then again, the Johnson we know is filtered through his acolyte and biographer, James Boswell, and what we read has been redacted accordingly. What it actually felt like to converse with him is said by those who knew him to have been a delightful experience—but still, we don't know if we would be equally delighted.

In the case of Johnson and his friends, as with many of the groups discussed below, what we know about the conversation, even if portions were (or professed to be) transcribed verbatim, is partial and biased by the reporter and, necessarily, taken out of a larger context. The "flow" of talk—of being swept up in the give-and-take of mutual exchange—is impossible to relay on the page, except metaphorically and artfully. Hence, the sketches below are to be taken less as statements of fact than as food for conversation in their own right. We can only guess what it felt like to be present in these situations with these people, and must decide for ourselves whether they would please our taste and sensibility.

Conversation as Instruction

I will discuss this later in connection to the college seminar, but for the sake of historical perspective, I want to single out the originary and most illustrious example of instructional conversation from antiquity. This happened at the so-called "Academy," founded in 387 BCE in Athens—the school established by Plato and central to the Western philosophical tradition. The teaching in this school followed the model of Plato's teacher, Socrates, whose method is recorded for us in Plato's dialogues where he features the persona of Socrates in conversation with his students and fellow citizens. The dialogues are a source of instruction on the full range of philosophical questions in the realms of epistemology, metaphysics, ethics, esthetics, and political science—in short, an entire college humanities curriculum.

Socrates's dialogues obviously involve dialogue, but they are not conversations in the equal and reciprocal sense in which we conventionally understand this. Socrates is asked a question and then proceeds to lead his interlocutor through a highly directed series of questions in response to that original question to arrive at something akin to an answer.

The nomenclature, "Socratic teaching," technically called the *method of elenchus* (which in Greek means "scrutiny"), refers to this process of arriving at "the truth." It sometimes is referred to as dialectical teaching under the assumption that it involves the thesis-antithesis-synthesis movement made famous by Georg Wilhelm Friedrich Hegel in his theory of intellectual history, and translated into economic terms by Karl Marx as the form of historical progress. It's also true that, in dialectical fashion, the Socratic method tends to lead from one question to another—that is, the synthesis splits again into interrogation and a later synthesis involving a new, temporary resolution. In its inability to find ultimate closure, it conforms with postmodern ideas about the eternal play of the signifier, though I doubt that Socrates would agree that truth is an ideological construct. Moreover, if the process conforms to Bakhtin's *dialogism*, it also works against that idea by ultimately subduing multiple voices rather than truly incorporating them. Socrates's impeccable gadfly logic takes precedence and nudges out the theories of his interlocutors, converting them to his position. In Plato's dialogues there is never any doubt as to who is the teacher and who the student. The hierarchy is maintained in both the form and the content of the interaction.

Here, for example, is an excerpt from Plato's most famous work, *The Republic*, on the topic of justice:

SOCRATES: . . . Should one also give one's enemies whatever is owed to them?

SIMONIDES: By all means, one should give them what is owed to them. And in my view what enemies owe each other is appropriately and precisely—something bad.

SOCRATES: . . . Now, what does the craft we call justice give, and to whom or what does it give it?

SIMONIDES: If we are to follow the previous answers, Socrates, it gives benefits to friends and does harm to enemies.

SOCRATES: Simonides means, then, that to treat friends well and enemies badly is justice?

This is obviously not an end point, and there follows a lengthy set of questions that lead to the revelation that many people don't know whether their friends are good or their enemies bad, leading the interlocutor to regroup and say, "It seems that we didn't define friends and enemies correctly." The dialogue then continues in a new direction as Socrates leads his audience to understand how justice should operate. At the end of Book 1, he asserts, "And so, Thrasymachus, injustice is never more profitable than justice." But though this is a declarative statement, it too is not an end point. The final lines of the dialogue take the subject in a new direction: "Hence the result of the discussion, as far as I'm concerned, is that I know nothing, for when I don't know what justice is, I'll hardly know whether it is a kind of virtue or not, or whether a person who has it is happy or unhappy."

We see that the exchange that we just read, as we embark on Book 2 of *The Republic*, was only a "prelude." Socrates will now take up the question of whether "it is better in every way to be just than unjust." The teaching proceeds, but the form has been established, which is to have Socrates direct and correct the others in a continual forward movement toward greater understanding. (Let me note here that *The Symposium*, which from its title would seem to be more egalitarian in its participants' conversation, follows the same Socrates-dominant style.)

There is something enervating about this line of inquiry for all its logical power and insight, and it is no wonder that Plato's dialogues are not to everyone's taste. Personally, I find that, as a teacher, I superficially adopt the method but also consciously work against it, trying to let students take me in directions that are unforeseen and force me to confront revelations that I may not have originally thought were true. I would call this not so much anti-Socratic as neo-Socratic, for I still occupy the role of teacher even as I open myself where I can to the novelty and insight that my students add to our interaction.

In this, I remain tied to the Western tradition epitomized by Plato's questions and answers. Recently, the tradition itself has been called to task for being, one could say, insufficiently "dialogic," in Bakhtin's terms—leaving out voices that ought to have been heard and hence creating a system of thought that supports the ruling class at the expense of the poor and marginal. I take this sort of broad-brush critique with a grain of salt, but I do think that if Western philosophy is epitomized by Plato, the limitations and blind spots of that tradition can be found in Socrates's style of teaching and that my own revision of it is at least a partial, if certainly incomplete, effort to amend it in Bakhtinian terms. I would go further and say that in conversation with friends—which is different from conversation in the classroom—the effort at dialogism is more successful. After all, I am not expected to teach anything—and the best conversations seek not to teach but to connect, illuminate, share, and extend meaning.

It must be said, moreover, that the Socratic dialogues do resemble the best sort of conversation in one respect: for all that Socrates is clearly in control of the proceedings and moves his students away from seeming misperceptions regarding key ideas, the dialogues themselves never reach a definitive end. There is always more to say, another topic to be broached, as one subject leads organically into another. In this respect, the dialogues model that sense of eternal possibility—of more material always waiting—that fuels the best sorts of conversations.

Plato's dialogues are themselves wonderful resources for conversation, even if one is not a philosopher or even a student of philosophy. If two people decide to read a few pages from *The Symposium* or *The Republic*, they can make it the subject of a dinner conversation that will lead in any number of surprising directions. Socrates can be the silent partner in that conversation, but by not being present, the connection between friends (perhaps even at times in opposition to that brilliant if irritating old man) can be a source of both hilarity and insight.

Conversation as Companionship

A different kind of conversation is one that hardly professes to have philosophical importance, though it frequently wanders into this territory. The thrust here is far more about fellowship than about teaching, however learned those involved may be.

The example of this that looms large in our Western cultural tradition involves that of the great eighteenth-century thinker and writer Samuel Johnson. Dr. Johnson and his friends met and conversed at the Literary Club in London, beginning in 1764 (and continuing after Johnson's death in 1784). The club originally consisted of a relatively small band of luminaries: the painter Joshua Reynolds (generally referred to as Sir Joshua Reynolds, since he was knighted in 1769), the poet and novelist Oliver Goldsmith, the historian and political philosopher Edmund Burke, and five others of lesser renown. The club later expanded to include such eminent figures as the actor David Garrick, the historian Edward Gibbon, and the economist Adam Smith.

The club was formed by Joshua Reynolds out of an act of friendship. Reynolds was concerned for Johnson's mental health. He knew that his friend's circumstances were sorely restricted by his low income and that Johnson was supporting a number of ne'er-do-well relatives and hangers on while being barely able to support himself. Reynolds's idea was to lift Johnson's spirits and make sure that he was properly fed at least once a week by having him engage with a group of friends every Friday evening at Turk's Head Tavern off the Strand. Reserved for this purpose was a private room, where the group ate and drank well into the night.

Reynolds made a point of inviting people from a variety of professions to join the Literary Club, which ensured that the conversation would range widely over art, literature, theater, and politics. I should note here that diversity was limited in other regards. Although most of the members were self-made and some, like Johnson and Goldsmith, were actually poor, they were an all-male, all-Christian (indeed all-Protestant) group. No woman, Jew, Catholic, or person of color was included, hardly surprising given the prejudices of the day. Johnson was also fiercely opposed to atheism and adamantly refused to meet the great philosopher David Hume, a professed unbeliever, despite the urgings of his friends to do so. (I would be unjust not to note that Johnson did enjoy conversation with women. His good friend and patron, Mrs. Thrale, engaged with him and a group of her friends regularly in what Leo Damrosch calls "a kind of shadow club." Nonetheless, it is the group that met at Turk's Tavern that has entered the annals of history as the apogee of companionate conversation.)

It is interesting for me to read about a group like this, one that seems so modern in so many ways, and realize that I would have been reflexively excluded from it. Yet I put this aside in recording my admiration for Johnson and his companions. If I start thinking in terms of past prejudices, I probably would never get any pleasure thinking about many things in history that I love. I believe that, as with conversation between different sorts of people in the present, we need to think about the past with the same generosity of spirit. Without condoning the kinds of prejudices and blindnesses that existed before, we ought to understand that they did not taint every element of the culture in which they existed (though I understand that some might think otherwise). Societies, like people, are not of a piece, and we often overlook negative characteristics in our friends in order to have them as friends and enjoy other characteristics that we love about them. My late friend Dave liked to cite the lines from the Woody Allen movie *Annie Hall* (now a problematic source in itself): "A guy walks into a psychiatrist's office and says, 'Hey doc, my brother's crazy! He thinks he's a chicken.' Then the doc says, 'Why don't you turn him in?' Then the guy says, 'I would but I need the eggs.'"

Dr. Johnson and many flawed individuals from the past strike me as deserving such consideration—"we need the eggs": the brilliant work they produced, despite their limitations and the limitations of their society. Boswell's *Life of Johnson* has been called the best biography ever written. I don't think this is quite accurate. Boswell's work is less of a biography in any conventional sense than it is an attempt to capture the conversation of a man with his friends in a medium that runs counter to the unpredictability and lived nature of conversation. Hence, the length and meandering style of the tome—and its originality; for it comes as close to bridging that unbridgeable divide between written record and conversation as one can get. Some sixty years after Boswell's work we would get a similar record—

this time of the conversation of the great German poet Johann Wolfgang von Goethe by his young personal secretary, Johann Eckermann. Eckermann could have been channeling Boswell's view of Johnson when he wrote, "We may, with propriety, compare this extraordinary mind and man to a many-sided diamond, which in each direction shines with a different hue. And as, under different circumstances and with different persons, he became another being, so I, too, can only say, in a very modest sense, this is my Goethe."

Boswell was similarly enamored of Johnson, and, in describing his friend in conversation with others, he is always represented as the first among equals. Was Johnson in fact so dominant on every occasion? There were other important intellects present—among them, Burke, the author of the monumental *Reflections on the Revolution in France*; Reynolds, who would become the first president of the Royal Academy of Arts; and later Smith, author of *The Wealth of Nations*. But Boswell was clearly biased and tilted the playing field in Johnson's direction. Still, it seems to me that group conversation (unlike conversation between two people) generally requires an orchestrating figure to keep it on track and to give it coherence. Johnson was such a figure. He was seen, not just by Boswell but by his other friends, as the most erudite man of his age, his conversation generally viewed as extraordinary. His friends conspired at one point to ensure that he had an ongoing stipend from the government to support him in whatever endeavor he chose to pursue (he had not had enough money to complete his studies at Oxford)—and this included having the leisure to attend the Literary Club at Turk's Head Tavern each week.

Boswell transcribes some of Johnson's conversations seemingly verbatim. The subjects touched upon are varied and arise unpredictably. In one instance Johnson breaks in on a discussion that has been proceeding about something else to talk about black bears:

> Johnson: "We are told, that the black bear is innocent; but I should not like to trust myself with him." Mr. Gibbon muttered, in a low tone of voice, "I should not like to trust myself with you." Boswell then concludes: "This piece of sarcastick pleasantry was a prudent resolution if applied to a competition of abilities."

A favorite topic was Johnson's scorn for Americans and their effort at independence: "I am willing to love all mankind except an American," Boswell quotes him as saying. He creditably noted the hypocrisy of men advocating for freedom while being slaveholders: "How is that we hear the loudest yelps for liberty among the drivers of negroes?"

Other topics include patriotism ("the refuge of a scoundrel," arguing that it is mostly a performance rather a reflection of true loyalty), happiness (man is never happy "but when he is drunk"), and other subjects as diverse as the value of getting one's wife a new dress and the function of Parliament. In most instances, Johnson seems to take the conservative position— he was a committed Tory and member of the Church of England—but his views are sometimes surprising; he does not always toe a party line.

Boswell made the recording of his friend's insights, aphorisms, and *bon mots* into his life's work and, more than that, his calling. He had a family at home in Edinburgh, but he was repeatedly drawn back to London where Johnson resided to be with his friend and spur him to engage in conversation. He loved their intimate meetings, but he also sought to bring people he admired into the fold so as to watch how Johnson conversed with them.

If you read *The Life of Johnson*, you see that though Boswell places himself below Johnson in status and intellect and makes no secret of the fact that he worshipped his older friend, he nonetheless records situations in which his presence is a necessary driver of their conversation. Consider this exchange where Boswell brings up the subject of why a mutual friend has become very fat; Johnson replies,

> "He eats too much, Sir." Boswell: "I don't know, Sir, you will see one man fat who eats moderately, and another lean who eats a great deal." Johnson: "Nay, Sir, whatever may be the quantity that man eats, it is plain that if he is too fat, he has eaten more than he should have done. One man may have digestion that consumes food better than common; but it is certain that solidify is increased by putting something to it." Boswell: "But may not solids swell and be distended?" Johnson: "Yes, Sir, they may swell and be distended; but that is not fat."

Note how Boswell both instigates the conversation and prolongs it with his strategic rejoinders.

Here are a few more examples of this type:

Boswell: "I understand [the poet Thomas Gray] was reserved, and might appear dull in company; but surely he was not dull in poetry." Johnson: "Sir, he was dull in company, dull in his closet, dull every where. He was dull in a new way, and that made many people think him Great. He was a mechanical poet."

Boswell: "You did not know what you were undertaking [in deciding to write the first English Dictionary]." Johnson: "Yes, Sir, I knew very well what I was undertaking,—and very well how to do it,—and have done it very well."

Boswell: ". . . A worthy friend of ours has told me that he has often been afraid to talk to you." Johnson: "Sir, he need not have been afraid, if he had any thing rational to say. If he had not, it was better he did not talk."

These highly amusing exchanges make clear that Boswell is "setting up" Johnson. He knows his friend, likes to goad him, and wants to see his preconceptions about Johnson's ideas reinforced and elaborated upon in original and amusing ways.

These exchanges strike me as resembling a stand-up routine (a performance metaphorically akin to the Abbott and Costello routine that I will discuss in chapter 8) rather than the kind of conversation that we value privately with friends. Yet I do think that, when engrossed in conversation at his London club, Johnson had the capacity to subdue his impulse to predominate and enter more equally into discussion with his friends who were erudite personalities with strong opinions of their own. Indeed, there is a current of camaraderie and fun that percolates through Boswell's biography; one feels how much he and others have genuine affection and respect for Johnson, which means that Johnson must have shown them affection and respect in turn.

Conversation as Creative Inspiration

One could argue that what we call a cultural "movement" is based on the idea that a group of people are creatively nurtured by prolonged conversation with each other. In other words, a group's conversation can become so reified for its creative glamour as to appear to direct the esthetic development of the society in which it exists.

The British Romantic Movement is an example of this. We tend to associate it with a certain kind of mindset that perme-

ated early nineteenth-century Western society. One thinks of
the Romantics as a communal whole, uniformly entranced
with the natural world and with feeling and imagination, a re-
joinder and even a refutation to the Enlightenment ideas that
preceded them. But the group was not as unified as has been
made out, and preoccupations as well as style varied among
those who have been dubbed Romantic poets (poetry being
the genre in which Romanticism was said to be essentially reflected). Nonetheless, there was a certain coherence to these
writers, at least in certain clusters, that had an outsized influence on their culture.

The Romantic Movement is often identified with the so-
called Lake Poets. These were principally William Wordsworth
and Robert Southey (the latter, more prose writer than poet),
who both had houses in this part of Northwest England. Dorothy Wordsworth, Wordsworth's sister, also a poet, lived with her
brother at Dove Cottage, Grasmere, in the Lake District, and
Samuel Taylor Coleridge visited for an extended period. This
group occasionally entertained others loosely associated with
it: the Shakespeare popularizers and essayists Charles and Mary
Lamb (who were also brother and sister); the memoirist, essayist, and notorious opium addict Thomas De Quincey; and several lesser known fiction writers and poets. The other famous
Romantics, Percy Bysshe Shelley, John Keats, and George Gordon,
Lord Byron, whom I will discuss below, were not part of this Lake
Poet group (both Keats and Shelley visited briefly but were not
drawn to the area). Shelley, Keats, and Byron were also part of
a younger generation of Romantics (though all three were dead
long before Wordsworth and Coleridge).

Coleridge moved to the Lake District in 1799 to be near
Wordsworth and remained there until 1804. The two men produced, together, the first published edition of their poetry,

Lyrical Ballads, for which Wordsworth wrote the preface that became a kind of manifesto for Romantic poetry. As with many close friendships, there seems to have been a division of labor that worked well until it ceased to do so. Coleridge was loquacious and theoretical; Wordsworth, taciturn and grounded. In their coauthored publication, they announced that they had divided their focus accordingly. In his 1817 *Biographia Literaria*, Coleridge explains their intention as follows: "My endeavours should be directed to persons and characters supernatural, or at least romantic, . . . Mr. Wordsworth on the other hand was to propose to himself as his object, to give the charm of novelty to things of every day." This has been popularly translated: Wordsworth sought to make the familiar strange; Coleridge, the strange familiar. We don't want to press this pat division of their respective intentions too far except to say that one can imagine how, in conversation, they would have enjoyed delineating and elaborating on it.

Complementarity works in conversation so long as it doesn't escalate into polarizing conflict. Keeping the differences under control, making them more piquant than confrontational, is at the root of good conversation in such cases. Yet the balance is a hard one, and it seems that Coleridge and Wordsworth could not maintain it. The inevitable falling out happened because their complementary relationship was also hierarchical— Wordsworth placed himself above Coleridge, who, initially, submitted to this placement but eventually felt himself to be eclipsed and his poetic style misrepresented or impugned (as he explains, not very clearly, in the *Biographia*).

It seems to me that the claim made by Wordsworth in the preface to the *Lyrical Ballads* that the poetry was "in the language really used by men" was a statement about his personal desire to strip away the pretention and artifice of previous poetry but also to try to inject into poetry some of the naturalness of conversation as he had experienced it, for a time, with Coleridge. Unfortunately, once Coleridge left the area, Wordsworth's poetry declined. Some might argue that the decline was a function of his increasing isolation from any kind of creative interaction. (The interactions with his sister and his wife seem to have been more idolatrous than reciprocal.)

As for Coleridge, one of this figure's great admirers was John Keats, who records a chance meeting he had with the older poet in 1819 and then walking with him for two miles during which they talked about a wide range of subjects: "let me see if I can give you a list—Nightingales, Poetry—on Poetical Sensation—Metaphysics—Different genera and species of Dream—Nightmare"—Keats's list goes on. Coleridge, however, records the meeting as lasting "a minute or two," noting only that there was "death in [Keats's] hand" when he shook it in bidding him goodbye. It seems likely to me that Coleridge, a relentless monologist, went on for an hour that seemed like a minute (to him) without engaging with his companion and hence without memory of the young poet beyond his tubercular hand. It is noteworthy that Coleridge published a collection titled *Table Talk* that ranged across such topics as "Americans," "euthanasia," "flogging," "keenness and subtlety," "differences between stories of dreams and ghosts," and "Homeric heroes in Shakespeare"—a compendious assortment that provides a glimpse, I think, into his conversational style (i.e., his tendency to run on learnedly without coming up for air). Keats apparently enjoyed listening to these brilliant meanderings, but I suspect some people were less indulgent.

But to return to Wordsworth. Jump ahead fifteen years, following his sojourn with Coleridge in the Lake Country. A history painter and member of the Royal Academy Benjamin

Robert (B. R.) Haydon decided to hold a gathering in Wordsworth's honor, since he was by now a venerated figure. Keats,
Lamb, and some half dozen others of some fame were invited
to attend. Referred to as the Immortal Dinner, this event is
worth discussing because Hayden kept a diary in which he described the conversation among his guests:

> Wordsworth was in fine cue, and we had a glorious set-to—
> on Homer, Shakespeare, Milton and Virgil. Lamb got ex-
> ceedingly merry and exquisitely witty; and his fun in the
> midst of Wordsworth's solemn intonation of oratory was like
> the sarcasm and wit of the fool in the intervals of Lear's pas-
> sion. . . . It was delightful to see the good humour of Words-
> worth in giving in to all our frolics without affectation and
> laughing as heartily as the best of us.

I am charmed by the image here of the gadfly Lamb engaging
with the solemn Wordsworth, though I'm not sure that I would
find what I suspect was Wordsworth's condescension as delightful as Haydon does.

The diary relays the topics of conversation at the dinner, the
kinds of questions that were asked, and the general temper of
the evening, which included a definite pecking order with respect to the participants, Wordsworth being unequivocally the
most august of the group.

It is hard to see this as an ideal conversation, no less an Immortal Dinner—indeed, it seems to have been a vanity event
for Haydon and a trussed-up tribute to Wordsworth. The former would commit suicide in 1846; the later would go on to
become poet laureate and live longer than anyone else present.
Keats would die in 1821, only a few years after the dinner. Lamb,
who would die in 1834, was perhaps a better conversationalist
than any of the others—and certainly the most fun. He and his

sister Mary entertained regularly at their modest abode in London. They lived together, except for the periods when Mary was admitted to a mental asylum for her bouts of insanity (in one fit she stabbed their mother to death).

The sibling relationships of the Lambs and of William and Dorothy Wordsworth were intense and enduring. They suggest to me that it was particularly hard for these creative people to make the passage out of the closed family of origin, and that their positioning both inside and outside their original family may have fed their creativity in some essential way. This seems to have been a Victorian dynamic. Charles Dickens, the quintessential Victorian novelist, makes brother-sister relationships (or rather brotherly-sisterly relationships) the only site of real intimacy and happiness for the protagonists in his novels.

The other cluster of Romantics who engaged in intensive conversation were very different in personality and lifestyle: Percy Bysshe Shelley, his wife Mary Shelley (formerly Mary Godwin), and the inimitable Lord Byron were the core participants. We see this group, along with Mary's half-sister Claire Claremont, having encounters together in various combinations that were often tempestuous and sexually charged. In one famous instance, the Shelleys, Byron, and Byron's physician, John Polidori, gathered in Geneva on a stormy Sunday, determined to entertain themselves. Unable to take the sailing expedition they had planned (the Romantics seemed to generally have a propensity for water—in the case of Shelley, an infelicitous one, since he ended up drowning), they began a lively discussion of galvanism, inspired by the lightning outside. As Mary recalled in her 1831 preface to *Frankenstein*,

Many and long were the conversations between Lord Byron and Shelley to which I was a devout but nearly silent listener.

During one of these, various philosophical doctrines were discussed, and among others the nature of the principle of life, and whether there was any probability of its ever being discovered communicated.

Interestingly, the two least involved in the conversation were spurred to write important works as a by-product of the encounter: Mary Shelley wrote *Frankenstein* and John Polidori *Vampyre* (a book that influenced Bram Stoker's *Dracula*). One wonders if Mary's work and, to a lesser degree, Polidori's were a response to being left out of the conversation of the two more powerful and illustrious personalities. I often think that writing is the way some people take unconscious revenge for being sidelined or not given their due in a lived context. (I was recently reminded of the Irish saying, "An Irish writer is a failed talker.") In the case of certain authors, the retreat into writing may reflect a certain megalomania that is unsatisfied with whatever obeisance they receive; they want to fully and completely control the conversation, possible only by committing their ideas to paper. In this sense, a written work represents the stubborn refusal of reciprocity that conversation, if any good, requires.

Daisy Hay, in writing about Shelley and Keats, makes the provocative observation that both were buried alongside a less illustrious friend: Shelley near Edward John Trelawny and Keats near Joseph Severn. Shelley and Keats, along with Byron, seem to have been attached to the idea of the poet as a solitary figure (a common Romantic trope), yet all three were often in company with others, traveling and living in sometimes communal fashion. Their placement in death beside a friend testifies to how important the lived connection must have been, both in nourishing their art and in giving them companionship and conversation outside of it.

Conversation as Avant-Garde Expression

The group that comes to mind immediately when we think about this sort of gathering is the Bloomsbury Group that gathered in that section of London near the beginning of the twentieth century. This group is singular not only in that it produced quite an array of significant works but also because it positioned itself squarely against the ideas and the general temper of the era that came before. The Romantics developed their respect for feeling and imagination against the rationalist bias of the Enlightenment that preceded them, but they did not feel the kind of disdain that the "Bloomsberries," as they called themselves, felt for their predecessors, the Victorians.

The Bloomsbury Group were made up mostly of graduates from Cambridge University (some had been members of the intellectual discussion group known as the Apostles, also dubbed the Converzatione Society). They met, at least initially, at the home of a former Apostle, Thoby Stephen, son of the writer Leslie Stephen and brother to the two sisters who would be known to posterity by their married names, Vanessa Bell and Virginia Woolf. After Thoby died in 1906, the group expanded somewhat, especially after Vanessa and Virginia married.

The Bloomsbury Group was intent on breaking with the conventions of the past and finding new kinds of subject matter both for conversation and for writing and art. In Vanessa Bell's memoir of her sister, she recalls that, as young children, Virginia "suddenly asked me which I liked best, my father or mother." Vanessa goes on, "Dimly some freedom of thought and speech seemed born, created by her question." That one could ask such a question, in other words, was a novelty that had not occurred to Vanessa or, one could argue, to the society she inhabited until her sister posed it.

A Bloomsbury regular, Gerald Brenan, refers to Virginia Woolf's "cascade of words like the notes of a great pianist improvising" and enumerates her favorite topics: "the Older Generation v. the Younger . . . Writers v. Painters or even Men v. Women." These are the kinds of conventional binaries that I noted in chapter 5 appeal to the French as a starting point for original observation. Likewise, Brenan notes, "It is these well-worn topics that produce the most brilliant and fantastic conversation."

Virginia Woolf famously proclaimed in her essay "Mr. Bennett and Mrs. Brown" that "on or about December 1910 human nature changed." She was referring to a far-reaching change in human relations that affected art in its connection to life: Writers like John Galsworthy and Arnold Bennett, Edwardians still linked to the earlier, Victorian age, she notes, "developed a technique of novel-writing which suits their purpose; they have made tools and established conventions which do their business." But the new writers like herself, James Joyce, and T. S. Eliot, whom she refers to as Georgians (and whom we would call "modernists"), are different: "Those tools are not our tools, and that business is not our business. For us those conventions are ruin, those tools are death."

If the conventions and tools of an earlier age were ruin and death to Woolf and her friends, the tools associated with "modernism" were new, and so was the conversation that followed from them. The Hogarth Press, overseen by Woolf and her husband Leonard, was the first to publish Sigmund Freud in translation by James Strachey, younger brother to Bloomsbury regular Lytton Strachey. At one of their gatherings in 1908, Lytton (who would write the great send-up of the luminaries of his parents' generation, *Eminent Victorians*) famously pointed to a stain on Vanessa Bell's dress and said bluntly, "Semen?" "With that one word," wrote Woolf of the incident, "all barriers of reticence and reserve went down. A flood of the sacred fluid seemed to overwhelm us. Sex permeated our conversation. . . . It was, I think, a great advance in civilization."

Reading about this incident, I am struck by how much it resembles, in form, Virginia Woolf's question to her sister when they were children. Both involved broaching formerly taboo subjects. They reflect the emergence of a cultural zeitgeist where new kinds of questions could be asked. One feels the excitement of what it must have been like to live at that time of disruption and innovation.

By the same token, I should note that there are trends in what is permissible in conversation, and this is not always a linear progression. Lytton Strachey's comment may have opened up new subject matter for discussion that seemed, as Woolf put it, "a great advance in civilization." But today, his remark might well have gotten him thrown out of the room or hauled into HR. In other words, what was an advance in that earlier era seems regressive if we widen the lens and think about it in another context—for example, how it relates to certain assumptions attached to male privilege. Feminist though she was in many respects, Virginia Woolf was not attuned to this particular way of understanding the question and was taken, instead, by its iconoclastic nature.

In fact, Woolf was unique in holding her own in gatherings where much of the talk centered around the men, especially in the early days of the group. The dominant players were Thoby Stephen's university friends: Strachey, art critic Clive Bell, economist John Maynard Keynes, and publisher Leonard Woolf. (Male dominance was even more pronounced within other avant-garde groups of the period like the Surrealists and the Dadaists.)

It is a truism that those who were avant-garde or progressive in some respects are often reactionary in others. We can never quite know what our blind spots are at any given time, which should make us more forgiving with respect to the past. We can also be assured that if we wait long enough, what was once avant-garde will cease to be so as it passes from the vitality of lived experience into the annals of history.

Conversation by Americans Abroad

Paris in the 1920s was a site of artistic congregation and, with it, of lively conversation—a fact helped by the kind of life I have described in chapter 5 as endemic to that city: the plethora of cafés and the style of discourse modeled by the French. For American expatriates, it became associated with a place, the Shakespeare and Company bookstore run by Sylvia Beach on the Rue de L'Odeon and dubbed "Shakespeare on Odeon" by James Joyce, who, though Irish, was part of the group that included the Americans Ernest Hemingway, F. Scott Fitzgerald, Ezra Pound, Sinclair Lewis, Thornton Wilder, and Sherwood Anderson. Joyce, it might be noted, was on the periphery of the Bloomsbury Group as well.

Beach held readings in her bookshop that were followed by talk. Other major places of congregation included the Café Flore, Harry's Bar, and the home of writer and patron Gertrude Stein, who lived there with her seemingly timid partner Alice B. Toklas. (Hemingway's report of overhearing a snippet of these women's private interaction is revelatory about how intimate conversation can diverge from its public form.)

In *A Moveable Feast*, Hemingway's memoir of the period (that he acknowledges could be taken as fiction), he recounts various conversations he had with his peers. Here, for example,

is a conversation he describes with his then-wife Hadley after
he discovered Sylvia Beach's bookstore:

> "We're going to have all the books in the world to read and
> when we go on trips we can take them."
> "Would that be honest?"
> "Sure."
> "Does she have Henry James too?"
> "Sure."
> "My," she said. "We're lucky that you found the place."

This follows on the heels of a similar conversation about what
they plan to have for lunch. The dialogue is painfully banal—
interesting not as a record of conversation but as an innovative
exercise in style. We would now call it "Hemingwayesque" in its
mannered minimalism, and it probably had no bearing on what
the actual conversation was like.

Hemingway devotes a considerable amount of space in his
memoir to his conversations with Gertrude Stein: "It was easy
to get into the habit of stopping in at 27 rue de Fleurus late in the
afternoon for the warmth and the great pictures and the conversation." They talk about writing and publication (according to
Hemingway, she was original but lazy), the purchase of art (she
tells his wife to give up buying clothes if they want to buy art),
and about other people, in mostly malicious terms. It seems that
for Hemingway (as for many young creative people in Paris
then), conversation with Gertrude Stein was useful to his development as a writer. By the time he falls out with her (which he
claims most of his peers also did), he has found his footing and,
one could postulate, no longer needs their talk. He does not give
us any concrete evidence for the way Stein's conversation was
motivating and inspiring, though he notes that people published
her work based on her scintillating conversation: "[They] took

on trust the writing of hers that they could not understand because of their enthusiasm for her as a person, and because of their confidence in her judgment."

One is tempted to wonder how being abroad—and particularly in Paris—allowed Stein to wield the power she did, and how the positioning outside one's country but within a group of compatriots may have empowered Hemingway to develop his uniquely "American" style of writing. One is also tempted to postulate how expatriatism connects to the need to break out of a familiar lexicon, involving one's country as well as one's family of origin. This was certainly the case for an earlier expatriate, Henry James, who, after a brief trial in Paris, settled definitively in London, where he dined out regularly with friends, both English and American (not to mention Italian, French, and Russian), and where he seems to have gained energy and ideas through his conversations with these different sorts of people. For James, conversation often provided the initial ideas for his novels and stories, though he was also explicit about how important it was that these "germs" be removed quickly from a real-world context in order to develop as fiction.

Conversation among Minority Americans in the United States

Paris would also attract African American artists during this period, most notably Countee Cullen, Claude McKay, Alain Locke, and Langston Hughes. These writers spent time in France with the expatriate group above but are more associated with the so-called Harlem Renaissance back home. For many

Black artists and intellectuals, Harlem came to occupy the same kind of perch on American society that Paris did.

The neighborhood in Upper Manhattan known as Harlem was initially a white middle-class enclave but opened to Black residents when developers realized that it had been overbuilt in the teens and 1920s. As a result, restrictions that existed elsewhere in the city were lifted and it became, in the words of Black writer and activist James Weldon Johnson, "the Negro capital of the world." It was the headquarters of the NAACP, the National Urban League, and Marcus Garvey's United Negro Improvement Association, and of newspapers and magazines specifically geared to a Black audience. The level of artistic activity in Harlem in the 1920s was spectacular. The Harlem YMCA (still in existence near the 135th Street subway station) was where the Harlem Writers' Workshop met and where figures like Langston Hughes and Claude McKay gave lectures to large and enthusiastic audiences. It was also where less prominent figures lodged and engaged in conversation.

Some say the Harlem Renaissance was launched by a dinner on March 21, 1924—more of an immortal one than that hosted by Haydon for Wordsworth in 1817. It was called the Civic Club Dinner, organized by sociologist and civil rights activist Charles Johnson and designed to bring white and Black writers together. The guest list was impressive and included such prominent white figures as the gadfly journalist H. L. Mencken, the businessman-turned-art-collector of Impressionist and African art Albert Barnes, and the playwright Eugene O'Neill. Among the Black intelligentsia present were W. E. B. Du Bois, Countee Cullen, Gwendolyn Bennett, Walter White, and Alain Locke. Some say that the conversation at the Civic Club Dinner was an impetus for the flowering of creativity that followed; others saw the dinner as evidence that the movement was beholden—and hence, inhibited—by white patronage. This continues to be a subject of debate.

Langston Hughes, in his memoir *The Big Sea*, talks about the parties at white patron Carl Van Vechten's apartment that "were so Negro that they were reported as a matter of course in the colored society columns, just as though they occurred in Harlem instead of West 55th Street." Hughes reports some incidents that occurred and *bon mots* exchanged (Van Vechten once held a "gossip party" in which guests were expected to tell the worst things they had heard about each other). In general, Hughes was quite comfortable in this milieu and wrote about Van Vechten appreciatively: "He never talks grandiloquently about democracy or Americanism. Nor makes fetish of those qualities. But he lives them with sincerity—and humor."

But this was far from everyone's viewpoint. One of the more biting representations of the Harlem Renaissance is in the fictionalized autobiography *Infants of the Spring*, by Black writer Wallace Thurman. In a chapter titled "Harlem Salon," he describes a meeting of all the notable Black artists and intellectuals of the day (thinly disguised under pseudonyms), where Dr. A. L. Parks (based on Dr. Alan Locke, the major champion and intellectual touchstone for the movement and editor of the *New Negro*) presides over a conversation about Black culture with respect to both its African roots and the white society in which it is situated. It is a complicated and nuanced conversation, but it ultimately satirizes many of the aspirations (Thurman might say "pretensions") associated with the group. Some of this satire pertains specifically to the positioning of Black artists in white America, but some of it could be leveled against any group that conceived of itself as an important cultural movement and hence became stuck in a static image of itself.

Conversation as Self-Promotion

If the Harlem Renaissance was happening uptown in Manhattan, another group of creative people were meeting weekly for lunch in midtown—at the Algonquin Hotel at East Forty-Fourth Street. The Algonquin Round Table, as it was called with obvious allusion to the Arthurian Round Table, was also known as the Vicious Circle, suggesting that its repartee was not particularly genial or kind.

The group was made up of initially lesser-known critics, writers, and playwrights who, through strenuous promotion and a modicum of talent, became famous in large part for being famous—for their wit in conversation as it was recorded mostly by themselves. Notable members included satirist Robert Benchley, columnist and sportswriter Heywood Broun, playwrights Marc Connelly, George S. Kaufman, and Robert E. Sherwood, critic and writer Dorothy Parker, and critic and journalist Alexander Wolcott. Another notable member was Harold Ross, described by Wolcott as looking like "a dishonest Abe Lincoln," who launched, midway through the decade, a new magazine called the *New Yorker*, where he published many of his Algonquin friends. The most important purveyor of the group's wit was Franklin P. Adams, who had a column in various publications of the day where he regularly cited his friends. The focus was on pithy statements more than on any sort of extended conversation, but these remarks were used to suggest that there was more where that came from. It glamorized the notion of improvisational chatter by clever people.

Not everyone was convinced, however. H. L. Mencken criticized the group as "trashy vaudevillians," and James Thurber, who lived in the hotel and so had a firsthand view (or, rather, ear), described them as mere pranksters rather than genuine creative people. Even Dorothy Parker, a prominent member whose quips were widely publicized, was harsh in her assessment: "There was no truth in anything they said. It was the terrible day of the wisecrack, so there didn't have to be any truth."

Here is a sampling of some of the members' famous remarks:

EDNA FERBER: "Being an old maid is like death by drowning, a really delightful sensation after you cease to struggle."

ALEXANDER WOOLLCOTT: "All the things I really like to do are either immoral, illegal or fattening."

GEORGE S. KAUFMAN: "Epitaph for a dead waiter—God finally caught his eye."

DOROTHY PARKER (when asked to use the word "horticulture" in a sentence): "You can lead a whore to culture, but you can't make her think." And (one of my favorites, having worn very short skirts in my day): "If you wear a short enough skirt the party will come to you."

FRANKLIN P. ADAMS: "The trouble with this country is that there are too many politicians who believe, with a conviction based on experience, that you can fool all of the people all of the time."

Some of these statements have also been attributed to others, and most of them are not, upon consideration, as clever as they are supposed to be. It seems you had to have been there—which is generally true of conversation. What makes wit seem so witty is that it appears in the midst of conversation rather than devised after the fact as *l'esprit de l'escalier* (as Milton Wright would put it). Some have suggested that the remarks were often developed ahead of time and sprinkled into conversation as needed. Regardless of how they were generated, the group's statements helped bolster their reputation for wit that has endured into the present.

In reality, this kind of talk is hard to maintain and is likely to burn itself out. In the case of the Round Table, the group had dissolved by the end of the 1920s.

Conversation around a Publication

One group of famous conversationalists who had far-reaching influence on American culture in the thirties and forties (though perhaps less far-reaching than they thought) were known as the New York Intellectuals or the *Partisan Review* Crowd because they so often published in that now-defunct journal.

Partisan Review began as a communist magazine founded by the John Reed Club and edited by Philip Rahv and William Phillips. It evolved into a progressive, intellectual journal treating arts, culture, and politics. As conversationalists, those attached to the journal—of whom we have a record from several memoirs by the participants—were convinced that they had cornered the market on insightful social commentary and criticism.

Though sometimes referred to as the American Bloomsbury, the *Partisan Review* Crowd could not have been more different in their backgrounds. The former were English upper-middle-class, Church-of-England people, educated at Oxbridge, while the latter were mostly first-generation Jews who had grown up in the tenements of the Lower East Side or the outer boroughs of New York City and educated at the free City universities. Exceptions were Lionel Trilling, who attended Columbia University and was much touted for being the first Jew to receive tenure in its English department, and Norman Podhoretz, also a Columbia graduate who did a spell of graduate work in England at Cambridge.

The group consisted originally of such figures as art critics Meyer Schapiro and Clement Greenberg and essayists and literary critics Alfred Kazin, Podhoretz, Daniel Bell, Sidney Hook, Irving Howe, Trilling and his wife Diana, Phillips, and Rahv. Most were the product of Yiddish-speaking homes. A few notable members of the group were not Jewish but had some of the hardscrabble manner of their ethnic counterparts—in particular, Mary McCarthy and Edmund Wilson, who met at the *Review* and were married for seven turbulent years. (As an aside, I consider my father and mother modified New York Intellectuals: born to Jewish immigrants in Brooklyn, they attended City universities, were appropriately left-leaning, and were avid "culture vultures," in the parlance of the day. But they ended up in the bourgeois enclave of suburban New Jersey rather than the progressive Upper West Side.)

The *Partisan Review* Crowd all shared a boisterous, somewhat defensive aspect—a pugnacity that showed itself in dramatic encounters and resulted in occasional purges of members for reasons that conflated political missteps and personal animus. They were all incisive writers whose words had an influence on society hard for us to imagine today.

The group's gatherings at each other's apartments became the stuff of legend. All of these people were great conversationalists. According to Irving Howe, most had started out as "talkative little pishers" in their immigrant homes, though they were eager to assimilate into American "high" culture. They were exceptionally well read and deeply concerned about how America should define itself in the twentieth century, which also included finding their own place in American life where they felt themselves to be outsiders. The relationship to communism became more complicated after Stalin's brutal purges.

William Barrett, a late arrival to the group, in his account *The Truants*, represents the *Partisan Review* Crowd as engaged in a good deal of self-indulgent and, in some cases, self-deceiving talk. He notes the contradiction, for example, of their support for both modernist writing and Marxism. For all their outspokenness, it seems that there was an intellectual if not political party line that couldn't be breached.

What eventually destroyed the group was the disparity between what they said to each other in person and what they wrote about each other when given the chance to publish their ideas for posterity. If some people tend to be gentler in writing than in speech, for the *Partisan Review* Crowd, the temptation to be incisive and memorable often trumped the inclination to be diplomatic or kind to friends. It is odd to think that these people lacked a sense of how they would feel the next day when they partook of cheese fondue with the person they had skewered in print. Their behavior strikes me as anticipatory of some of the social media behavior we see today—where people will behave viciously online and politely enough in live interaction.

The most egregious example of published meanness occurred after Norman Podhoretz, a particularly vulnerable, if precocious, member of the group, published the memoir *Making It*, in which he presented himself as wanting the good things that America had to offer—that is, unabashedly seeking fame and fortune and implying that many of his friends at the *Partisan Review* felt the same way. This was apparently a déclassé thing to admit. The group was outraged and turned on him (or rather, on his book, which they excoriated). The biggest betrayal came from Podhoretz's best friend at the time, Norman Mailer, who actually told him he liked the book in person and then went on to savage it in the pages of *Partisan Review*. Podhoretz fell into a depression, broke with the group, and emerged some years later as a father of the neoconservative movement.

I asked Podhoretz in an interview whether there was a connection between his treatment and his revised politics, and he claimed there was not, but the pain that entered his voice when he spoke of Mailer and the response of the *Partisan Review* Crowd to his book (which I, incidentally, found to be honest, intelligent, and highly readable) was still palpable a half century later. Here was a living example of how the written word can calcify around an idea and eliminate the more human response that flourishes more naturally in conversation.

Conversation as Therapy

I have already said that I did not see therapy as authentic conversation because it has a utilitarian goal and is one-sided: the therapist interrogates the patient; the patient talks about herself. I make an exception, however, in the case of the therapeutic program known as Alcoholics Anonymous (AA). AA was launched in 1935 in Akron, Ohio, by two men, Bill Wilson and Dr. Bob Smith, generally referred to only by their first names, Bill and Dr. Bob, in keeping with the concern for anonymity that is a hallmark of the group. (The family home of Dr. Bob in Akron is now a museum and site of pilgrimage for those wishing to pay tribute to the group's origin story.)

I decided to include AA in this list of conversational groups after I spoke with a friend who is a longtime member. He explained that participants often engage in conversation that may not necessarily focus on their drinking. He pointed to three factors in the precepts of AA that account for the depth and intensity that can characterize this conversation: the need for radical honesty, the acknowledgment of human limitation, and the quest for moral virtue. These factors make it inevitable that conversation of a probing and wide-ranging sort will result.

Members must accept that their alcoholism is outside their control and submit their will to a "higher power" or to "God as we understand him"—wording that can encompass the agnostic and even the atheist. For my friend, the higher power constitutes the group itself: the support system that transcends the individual.

AA grew out of revivalist Christianity, and it incorporates a number of prescribed elements: it is built around twelve "steps," and there are ritualized readings and formats to many of the meetings. Yet one of its founders characterized it as "benign anarchy." There is no paid leader, and its organizations, which exist throughout the world, are self-supporting. It relies heavily on a system that, my friend explains, involves testimonials about the struggle with drinking but also encourages conversation about life's tribulations more generally.

As explained to me, AA creates the intimacy and support of friendship among people of vastly different backgrounds who all share in one weakness: an unhealthy dependence on alcohol. The goal is not only the singular one of healing but also the larger, existential one of acknowledging one's weakness as a human being and using this awareness to stop drinking. The expansive context in which the problem is placed is what makes conversation in AA so productive and often so profound. One can see how its loose, interactive structure would make it adaptable to many kinds of dependencies, which is why twelve-step programs now exist for drugs, food, sex, shopping, and no doubt more arcane kinds of addiction.

Conversation as Social Protest

If Harlem was the center of the genteel Harlem Renaissance of the 1920s, it also emerged as a more combative site of social protest in the sixties and seventies. Sylvia's Restaurant at East 125th Street was one of several meeting places around the country for activists. It helped that major student protests were taking place against the Viet Nam War not too far down the road at Columbia University. This was a period of tumult on behalf of social justice, in many ways akin to our current era. (During the same period, gay activism was also being spearheaded at the Stonewall Inn in Greenwich Village, when it was raided by police on June 28, 1969.)

Perhaps the most telling and dramatic example of a conversation that connects provocatively to the Civil Rights Movement is chronicled in James Baldwin's wrenching autobiographical essays in *The Fire Next Time*. Baldwin recounts a dinner he had at the home of Nation of Islam founder Elijah Muhammad on the South Side of Chicago. Here, he was confronted with a Black activist ideology that was in direct opposition to white society. Baldwin first describes the conversation in the room into which he is ushered before Muhammad arrives:

> Conversation was slow, but not as stiff as I had feared it would be. They [the adherents of the Nation of Islam] kept it going, for I simply did not know which subjects I could acceptably bring up. . . . We were all waiting for the appearance of Elijah.

He goes on to describe what happens after Muhammad enters and takes his seat at the table:

> Now [Elijah] turned toward me, to welcome me, with that marvelous smile. . . . I knew what he made me feel, how I was

drawn toward his peculiar authority, how his smile promised to take the burden of my life off my shoulders. Take your burdens to the Lord and leave them there.

Baldwin is drawn to Muhammad, but he is also put off by the style of the man's conversation and by the subservience and rote response of his adherents:

> Whenever Elijah spoke, a kind of chorus arose from the table, saying "Yes, that's right." This began to set my teeth on edge. And Elijah himself had a further, unnerving habit, which was to ricochet his questions and comments off someone else on their way to you.

Much of what follows involves Baldwin listening to the repeated observation that white men are devils. Despite his awareness of prejudice and his sympathy for many elements associated with the group, he cannot stomach this unnuanced expression of hatred, and ends by hurriedly taking his leave.

What Baldwin manages to do in this passage is render what it feels like to be present with true believers in a setting in which the political agenda is invoked at every turn. This is an extreme case of what I have felt in some instances in my own life, even when the subject matter is not overtly political but simply involves an implied agreement about how things are or should be. Even when I agree with what others are saying in the aggregate, I resent the assumption that I agree, or that there aren't areas that need more examination. In academia, in particular, there tends to be an elevated sort of faculty groupthink, so that even a seemingly casual conversation can end up feeling coercive.

By the same token, when ideas from radical groups filter into the mainstream, they often get softened, adjusted, and abridged, in which form they can truly affect the thinking of a large, general population and inspire change.

If the conversation with Elijah Muhammad is one extreme of a group conversation connected to the historic Civil Rights Movement, another is the dinner party for the radical Black Panthers, held in 1970 in the Upper East Side Manhattan apartment of the conductor and composer Leonard Bernstein and his wife Felicia Montealegre. That party was immortalized in savagely satirical terms in an essay, "Radical Chic: The Party at Lenny's," in *New York Magazine* by Tom Wolfe, one of the pioneers of the so-called New Journalism. Wolfe ridiculed the event as an example of wealthy and status-conscious people embracing fashionable political ideas. He emphasized the hypocrisy of the Bernsteins, who were entertaining a revolutionary group who were opposed to everything the couple stood for.

The Bernsteins might have explained that they were interested in conversing with people who, they felt, had a valid viewpoint on a society that they themselves had originally entered as outsiders. Bernstein, like the *Partisan Review* Crowd, came from an immigrant Jewish family and was bisexual; his wife was from Costa Rica and grew up in Chile. In short, despite their success, the couple's ability to connect with the Panthers might have been greater than was thought at the time. Filtered through Wolfe's unforgiving viewpoint, however, the gathering became a focus of ridicule and indignation. What might have been an opportunity for creative connection between unlike groups was flattened into a farcical spectacle.

What seems to have been central in many of the cases I discussed above was a place or set of places where the group could gather and talk on a regular basis, and which helped solidify their reputation *as* a group in the public imagination. Some of these gathering places have since been turned into commercialized sites, with souvenirs and references in guidebooks. Their status as tourist attractions exists in marked contrast to the spontaneous engagement that supposedly took place there.

Some additional places that fall into this category, along with those I have already mentioned, include Giverny outside of Paris (the Impressionists); El Quatre Gats café in Barcelona (Modernist artists); Les Deux Magots café in Paris (the Existentialists); Dooky Chase's Restaurant in New Orleans (jazz musicians), and the Cedar Bar (the Abstract Expressionist art movement), later rechristened the Cedar Tavern (the Beat poets). There are many more such sites where talented individuals gathered in conversation with like-minded peers. These gatherings often built the support and the confidence needed to create art.

There is a counterpoint to this idea, however. If good conversation can spur creative thinking, it can also be detrimental to creative productivity. Conversation is extemporaneous and communal; writing and painting are solitary and involve more control and discipline. The latter is harder than the former, and too much talk can dissipate the will to create.

For this reason, some artists have chosen to pull away from a group in an effort to conserve their talent. I have felt—and my informal survey of other writers supports the fact—that when I talk too much about an idea for a novel or essay, I find myself sapped of the desire to write it. Samuel Johnson, it is said, might have written more had he conversed less, and many of the Algonquin participants had more promise in their talk than what they were able to realize on paper. Edna Ferber, who was awarded the Pulitzer Prize in 1924, and playwright Robert Sherwood, who won multiple Pulitzers in the thirties and forties, felt the need to break with the Algonquin Round Table in order to find space—both time and mental energy—to write.

But then, who's to say that books or plays or paintings are better than conversation? While our modern notion of genius tends to favor the artistic product, the Romans (or at least Cicero) saw its most fertile expression in dialogue with others. It's true that the former leaves a record for posterity, but posterity happens when we have left the stage. And how do we know that we won't affect others in more important ways through conversation than through our scribbled attempts at music composition, poetry or prose, our dabbing on canvas or in the plastic arts?

The pleasures of convivial talk are hard to weigh against the fact of royalties and the prospect of being appreciated after death. Maybe it comes down to this question: Is it life or honor that we value more? I tend (at least sometimes) to favor the former, along with Shakespeare's Falstaff, for whom conversation, well lubricated with food and drink, won the contest every time.

CHAPTER 7

The Rise of the Novel—and Female Talk

While the French had a tradition of mixed-sex salons beginning in the seventeenth century, the English were devoted to gentlemen's clubs where, as one book on the subject put it, "a man goes to be among his own kind." The phrasing suggests both sex and class as elements of "kind," a delineation that may now make us wince in distaste and embarrassment.

But such clubs continued to flourish in England up through the middle of the twentieth century and even beyond. When I visited the Oxford and Cambridge Club in London in the early 1990s, I was asked to leave the front bar when I sat down there unknowingly; this room was still an all-male precinct (the club had allowed women members in 1972 but opened completely to women only in 1996). The Reform Club, named in honor of the supporters of the 1832 Reform Bill, began to admit women in 1981; the esteemed Atheneum Club in 2002. White's and Pratt's, elite aristocratic clubs, and the Garrick, a theatrical club named after the venerable Shakespearean actor David Garrick, continue to exclude women as members as of this writing. But a good indicator that these segregated, elite clubs are effectively obsolete is reflected in the fact that the phrase "gentlemen's club" has been usurped. Now when one hears the phrase, one thinks first of more prurient forms of entertainment that don't involve conversation.

The long-standing existence of the gentlemen's club (in its traditional manifestation) seems connected to the fact that England, perhaps more than any other Western country, had a tradition of "separate spheres" that went back to the early period of industrialization. From the seventeenth century up through the 1930s and 1940s, women in upper-class households were expected to leave the table after the dessert so that the men could share conversation unimpeded over cigars and cognac. One sees this enacted in old movies, even when set in America (for example, at the beginning of *Gone with the Wind*), and it can seem quaint and rather elegant until you actually focus on the reality: that the women are being shepherded away so that the men can converse "freely." What kind of inhibition did women denote, and what kind of talk did their presence inhibit?

And yet for all the power of patriarchal privilege, increased female influence and, with it, female discourse began to be felt in England and the rest of the Western world with the rise of the novel (here I would include France, insofar as the novel reached a wider, more democratic audience than the salons that had existed there since the seventeenth century). The genre pioneered an interest in a new subject matter and style of discourse and began, in an indirect way, to challenge patriarchy. According to some critics, it marked a "feminization" of culture that was seen to weaken the fabric of these nations; for others, it inspired an interest in middle-class domestic life and in the interior and emotive aspects of character.

The novel was a new kind of representational genre. It emerged in the West in the eighteenth century (though there

were stirrings in the seventeenth and before), a product of increased industrialization and urbanization, alongside a burgeoning, highly literate middle class. The form of the novel allowed
the author to describe the inner life of its characters through
descriptive narration, providing a more nuanced and exhaustive
sense of identity than that provided by other literary forms or by
the dramatic soliloquy in theater. This inner life is what, a
century later, Freud, no doubt influenced by a culture shaped by
the novel, would codify into a psychological theory.

The popularity of the novel also reflected what sociologist
Thorstein Veblen attributed to capitalistic expansion: middle-
class women became the emblems of their husbands' success
by having what he called "vicarious leisure." In other words, if
the men worked hard enough, they could afford to have their
wives *not* work. This idea persisted until well into the twentieth
century. I recall how, when I was a child, my father initially opposed my mother's insistence on working outside the home.
But he became acclimated to her career a few years later as
second-wave feminism began to gain support; and he was eventually proud of her position as the town's French teacher and
grateful for the income she earned since it allowed him to take
risks late in his own career that would otherwise have been
impossible.

Although "vicarious leisure" was denigrating to middle-class
women in barring them from the workplace and turning them
into evidence of their husbands' success, it had the compensa-
tory value of giving them large expanses of time in which they
could read (and in some cases write) novels—and talk with
each other about the characters and issues raised in them.

The genre also reflected a societal shift in the structure of
relationships: from the extended family to the nuclear family,
and from the arranged marriage to the companionate or "love"

marriage, making these new forms of relationship central to its plot lines. The nuclear family was the context in which the novel was set, and the heroine's passage out of that family of origin via the courtship plot drove the narrative forward. In this way, novels supported the cultivation of a female-oriented discourse that would have far-reaching effects on culture.

An important landmark in the history of the English novel was the work of Jane Austen, who produced six completed novels in the late eighteenth and early nineteenth centuries. Austen followed popular novelist Samuel Richardson, amending his male-inflected view of domesticity. She proceeded to take control of the genre, so to speak, and her influence on the form has only increased over time.

While Austen certainly had a following dating from the first publication of her work, she also had serious detractors who were put off by what they saw to be her overly feminine style and subject matter. While such ostensibly "masculine" writers as Walter Scott and Lord Byron admired her novels (Scott praised her "exquisite touch" against his own "Big Bow-wow strain"), Mark Twain and, later, H. L. Mencken did not (perhaps they saw her refined esthetic as an implicit challenge to their crude and youthful nation, which was beginning to flex its muscles on the world's literary stage). Twain is quoted as saying that when he read Austen he "[felt] like a barkeeper entering the Kingdom of Heaven."

Despite such criticism, Austen's popularity has increased, especially from the mid-twentieth century on, dating from when British critic F. R. Leavis included her in his *Great Tradition* of the English novel and American critic Lionel Trilling wrote several important essays about her.

If Leavis and Trilling made Austen acceptable in the academic world, movie and television adaptations extended her appeal. By the end of the twentieth century she had become hugely popular with the general public, making it possible for people to be familiar with her work without having actually read it.

Austen's burgeoning popularity in both the West and the East—when I visited China, I found she was popular there as well—seems in part a function of a greater willingness on the part of society to take women and their preoccupations seriously. Moreover, the mannerly dialogue that characterizes the interactions of her characters (that can be easily transferred to movies and television) is especially appealing in a world that seems increasingly angry and uncouth. Her novels supply something of a guidebook on how to discourse with civility when the people around you are at odds or incompatible.

Austen organized her novels around "three or four families in a country village" who meet each other again and again in various social situations. This is the ideal scenario for conversation. But though the novels describe a world in which people continually talk to each other, the conversation they engage in is not the free-flowing, spontaneous sort that I most admire—that Virginia Woolf evokes at her fantasy luncheon at Oxbridge and that Wallace Shawn and André Gregory engage in toward the end of their dinner together.

Instead, Austen is concerned with the difficulties posed by conversation. Some people have a hard time mastering how to talk properly; others deliberately use language duplicitously to trick or mislead those they engage with. This means that instruction is needed on two fronts: first, in how to speak properly and, second, in how to decipher character by scrutinizing actions as they may contradict or append words.

Austen's most famous novel, *Pride and Prejudice*, actually contains a tutorial in conversation by its heroine, Elizabeth Bennet, for its hero, Fitzwilliam Darcy. Darcy is the first type of impaired conversationalist. He seems to be a supremely eligible bachelor: rich, handsome, and a devoted friend and brother. However, he has not mastered the rules of conversational etiquette that would make him a proper consort for the heroine. He snubs her at the first dance they attend together; then he fails to make clear to her his growing interest. When they finally do dance together, she uses the occasion to satirize his behavior and to give him a lesson in conversation:

> After a pause of some minutes, she addressed him a second time with:—"It is *your* turn to say something now, Mr. Darcy. *I* talked about the dance, and *you* ought to make some sort of remark on the size of the room, or the number of couples."
>
> He smiled, and assured her that whatever she wished him to say should be said.
>
> "Very well. That reply will do for the present. Perhaps by and by I may observe that private balls are much pleasanter than public ones. But *now* we may be silent."
>
> "Do you talk by rule, then, while you are dancing?"
>
> "Sometimes. One must speak a little, you know. It would look odd to be entirely silent for half an hour together; and yet for the advantage of *some*, conversation ought to be so arranged, as that they may have the trouble of saying as little as possible."

Another exchange between Darcy and Elizabeth on the subject of conversation continues the lesson and clarifies what is at issue:

> "I certainly have not the talent which some people possess," said Darcy, "of conversing easily with those I have never seen before. I cannot catch their tone of conversation, or appear interested in their concerns, as I often see done."

"My fingers," said Elizabeth, "do not move over this instrument in the masterly manner which I see so many women's do. They have not the same force or rapidity, and do not produce the same expression. But then I have always supposed it to be my own fault—because I would not take the trouble of practising. It is not that I do not believe *my* fingers as capable as any other woman's of superior execution."

I believe that part of what so appeals to readers about this novel is the reversal of the conventional power relationship: the female character schools the male character in conversation and, subsequently, in the importance of practice in becoming adept at this social skill.

If, like Darcy, one can be awkward and unschooled in conversation, one can also be false in one's use of language. Another of Elizabeth Bennet's suitors is the clownish figure of William Collins. It's easy to recognize his shallowness and lack of moral character. But it can take time and attention to discern inconsistency and falsity in conversation when the individual is more duplicitous. Even though Elizabeth seems to be a discerning person, she is initially taken in by the smooth-talking George Wickham. Only after he has moved on to another woman and his treacherous past actions are revealed is she able to "hear" the hollowness of his talk.

Similar lessons connected to conversation are represented in Austen's other novels. In *Emma*, the heroine sees more in the rather shallow Frank Churchill than is there; inadvertently encourages the attention of the unctuous Mr. Elton; and fails to realize that her ideal consort, Mr. Knightley, is right there in front of her. By contrast, it is a tribute to the steadfast if rather dull character of Fanny Price, the heroine of Austen's *Mansfield Park*, that she is not taken in by her glib but unscrupulous suitor,

Henry Crawford. Part of the lesson of Austen's last novel, *Persuasion*, is that it often takes time to see clearly the value of another person, and that relationships should not be rushed. As Anne Elliot, the heroine, explains to her suitor, Captain Wentworth, whom she initially rejected but with whom she has been reunited after many years of separation, "I must believe that I was right [in the initial rejection], much as I suffered from it."

Austen's novels demonstrate that conversation is both a barrier and a bridge to understanding in a world that is structured and mannerly. Her characters engage in careful, deliberate talk so as to gradually make themselves known, assess who their conversants are, and decide whether they want to know them better. At intervals, they push against the boundaries of decorum: that "impertinence" with which Elizabeth interacts with Darcy and that he later explains is what attracted him to her. However, only after the marriage of heroine and hero has been achieved can we imagine them engaging in genuinely spontaneous and intimate talk. As the narrator explains on the last page of *Pride and Prejudice*, Georgiana, Darcy's young sister, "often listened with astonishment bordering on alarm at the lively, sportive, manner of [Elizabeth's] talking to her brother."

Austen frames one end of the domestic novel tradition by which Anglo-American culture has defined conversation; Henry James bookends it at the other end. James wrote at the turn of the twentieth century as an American expatriate in London. As I mentioned earlier, I believe that James needed to uproot himself from his family and his country in order to do his work—not only to be personally free from the inhibitions within which he had grown up but also to have a perspective from which he could think about the literary tradition he had inherited and where he might position himself, whether within or against it.

While Austen's characters hold to a more or less ritualized style of conversation that can be misleading or duplicitous, James's speak in opaque, fragmentary statements that require a different kind of attention.

The goals have shifted when we move from the end of the eighteenth century to the end of the nineteenth. In James, the feminization of culture that began with Austen has now opened up the possibility for greater influence by women on men than had existed earlier in the century. This poses a more complicated and, one could argue, greater creative challenge. In the preface to his 1881 *The Portrait of a Lady*, James had announced "how inordinately the Isabel Archers and the much smaller female fry insist on mattering." This idea of "women mattering" becomes more and more central to his work as he continues to write.

The quintessential novel of conversation in James's canon is his 1899 *The Awkward Age*. The product of his late "major phase," this often-enervating work is organized, as James explained in its preface, to resemble the five acts of a play, and is almost completely in dialogue. There is no "central intelligence" to filter the action, only the talk of the characters that we, as readers, must assess for what it says about their moral and emotional lives. Austen's use of dialogue was copious and sometimes misleading but always, ultimately, decipherable; James's is anything but. It is infuriatingly opaque and impossible to fully understand.

For me, James's work is the closest one can come to a novel where we as readers are part of the conversation—made to continually interpret the speech of the characters, which is never entirely clear or resolved, and which constantly throws us forward to new possibilities of meaning.

Moreover, *The Awkward Age* is especially relevant to my argument because it not only involves conversation among its characters but also is *about* conversation—talk as such is a special focus of concern for the characters and for the reader.

The novel centers on a group, presided over by the socially adept Mrs. Brooke, a latter-day salonnière. She and her friends—who call themselves the Brooke Circle—are concerned with how their talk may affect Mrs. Brooke's adolescent daughter, Nanda. Nanda is at the awkward age of the title: old enough to understand what is said but young enough to be "corrupted" by what she hears. Presumably, the "good talk" of her mother's circle is not unlike the talk of the Bloomsbury Group: full of sexual innuendo and illicit gossip—in other words, "bad talk" for an adolescent girl to hear. Nanda, as the characters note again and again, has been exposed to this talk by virtue of living under her mother's roof, unlike her counterpart, little Aggie, another of the regulars' daughters, who has been assiduously protected from it. At one point, the group learns that Nanda has read a novel left out on a table, and this seems to confirm her corruption—solidifying the relationship between the group's conversation and the subject matter of novels.

Nanda, as it happens, is in love with Vanderbank, a suave and cosmopolitan bachelor, who, for years, has been her mother's "property" (probably her lover, though James takes care not to be explicit on this score). For Nanda to take Van from her mother would not only be to take away her mother's most important relationship but also to symbolically dissolve the group. Thus, she is placed in the difficult position of having to work through her feelings for Van, for her mother, and for her role in society through the way she deals with Van.

At the end of the novel, Nanda leaves the group to be taken under the wing of an old, rich man, who appreciates her for herself and will remove her from the talk of her mother's friends.

He will also presumably assure her a sexless but comfortable future as his companion.

The contrast between Jane Austen and Henry James is striking, and yet there is a clear through line to be drawn between them. As stylistically different as they are, they both focus exclusively on domestic space and female-dominated conversation. Both are able to create an atmosphere in which words take on enormous power and require careful study and discrimination. We can see how Freud's "talking cure" pertains to these worlds (Vienna was not London, but it shared many of the same urban, modern characteristics). The more the characters talk, the more they reveal themselves, both to us, the reader, and to each other.

Both Austen and James have been denigrated in some quarters for being self-indulgent and cut off from the larger world. This fits the stereotype long associated with female conversation, often consigned to the background or disparaged for being trivial or silly. How often, even in recent history, has an implicit trivialization of a woman's role in a situation failed to take into account her potential influence or importance.

Such underlying sexism may explain why the early twentieth-century novel saw a revolt of sorts against female talk. The modernist novel introduced the innovation of stream of consciousness that put the drama inside the head of individual characters, hence reducing the need for conversation. A new literary esthetic also emerged that employed a more minimalist kind of representation (a "masculine" style embodied by Hemingway) and was reinforced with the emergence of cinema as the principal entertainment form of the twentieth century. Early movies were without simultaneous sound, but even after talkies arrived in the late 1920s, they remained primarily a dynamic visual medium. The Western, the quintessential American movie genre, focused on landscape and action; its hero, the cowboy, was the embodiment of rugged male inarticulateness.

The denigration of women as foolish and inconsequential in their talk is the by-product of this esthetic. Though countered in various parts of society and in various corners of representation (e.g., the "fast-talking dames" of thirties and forties screwball comedy), it has continued to prevail up through the recent past, if not into the present. A great deal was made, for example, of Nancy Reagan's influence on her husband, but no one seemed to think that whatever success is attributed to Reagan (said to be greater and greater as time passes) might be attributable to her. That Monica Lewinsky conversed with President Clinton, along with doing other things, was also never taken seriously.

Women's conversation is often denigrated as gossip. Gossip is conversation about someone not present, but such talk can be trivial and mean-spirited or focused on fine discriminations regarding behavior and character—indeed, it can be both. "Call it gossip if you will," notes Anne Elliot in Austen's *Persuasion* regarding another character, "but . . . she is sure to have something to relate that is entertaining and profitable, something that makes one know one's species better." Literary critic Patricia Meyer Spacks has taken Anne Elliot's cue, arguing that gossip is valuable in helping us learn more about each other and ourselves; it is also, she maintains, the very stuff of which the novel, with its interest in personality and the minutiae of daily life, is made. Yet the term still exists in a denigrating alliance with women. The *Gossip Girl* book series (made into two TV series), a hugely popular franchise involving New York City teenagers, indelibly brands young girls with the moniker of gossips.

Similarly, the phrase "ladies who lunch" evokes a group of capri-panted women, nails recently lacquered, hair coiffed, sitting in a country club or airy suburban restaurant, conversing about fashion and home décor. I have always found this nomenclature to be both sexist and generally inaccurate. Women do tend to congregate over meals to discuss both personal and more general topics. Many of these women hold important jobs but maintain social connections with other women who share their complex relationship to children, household, spouses, and work. Moreover, conversation about subjects like fashion and décor continues to be denigrated as somehow more trivial than conversation about sports and cars.

While the gendering of conversation may now be less common than it once was, it still exists by virtue of the fact that women and men tend to perform different roles in the family or have a different relationship to the same roles. Thus, when gathered in segregated groups, they engage in conversation that is different, if not in subject matter then in style and tone. Deborah Tannen has described this in her many books on this subject.

What we can do is recognize the prejudice that has long tended to elevate white male conversation over that of women and other traditionally marginal groups. Will these prejudices wither away as we become a more gender-neutral or gender-fluid society? Virginia Woolf was an early advocate for this idea when she extolled an androgynous future in which there would be no such thing as distinctively "women's" writing (and by extension, I assume, as women's talk). However, as we begin to acknowledge the value of female and minority interests and related styles of expression, the idea of androgyny has taken on more ambiguous value. The hope is not to dilute difference but to converse across it and have it enrich and enliven our conversation.

CHAPTER 8

Conversation as Public Entertainment

Both Jane Austen and Henry James were able to create the illusion that their characters were engaged in "real" conversation, though each chose a different means of doing so. Austen created a highly mannered form of public expression, leading, presumably, to more spontaneous, intimate conversation outside the parameters of the novel. James used fragments and suggestive words and phrases, leaving us to imaginatively fill in what is not said. In both cases, the reader is carried forward in the hope of arriving at something that is never represented directly.

The indirection by which these great novelists approached conversation helped teach me how to write dialogue in my own fiction. I had previously tried to copy real speech in my efforts at novel and short story writing; the result was wooden and boring. When I finally stopped copying and approached dialogue more artfully, it became, ironically, more seemingly natural as well as more entertaining.

A breakthrough example can be found in my first published novel, *Jane Austen in Boca,* a satirical comedy of manners with a high-concept plot: "*Pride and Prejudice* set in a Jewish retirement community in Boca Raton, Florida," as my publicist put it. The scene in question takes place in the dining room of the retirement complex where a group of young cinematographers have arrived to film the elderly residents. Here's how the scene eventually read:

At lunch on the Friday of the first week of filming, the group had positioned itself in what seemed to be relative seclusion at the end of the buffet table. George was holding the camera and Jordan the boom mike, and Amy had gotten hold of a man in pink Bermuda shorts and asked him to speak a little about his interests.

"Interests? What interests?" exclaimed the man irritably, as though he had been asked to discuss his bank account or his sex life.

"How can I have interests? Once Leona passed, my interests were kaput." The man snapped his fingers and continued in a less irritable tone. "We had interests together. We were best friends." He sighed resignedly. "It's like having your arm cut off. Not here"—he indicated the elbow—"but here"—he pointed to his shoulder. "It's walking around without an arm."

"Don't I know," noted a woman in a sequined jogging suit who had sidled into the conversation while getting herself more potato salad. "Jack and I did everything together. But you make do. The children are always asking: 'How do you spend your time?' I tell them that I find occupation."

"They're running around getting degrees, networking," continued the man, taking up from the jogger's point about children. "I tell them: 'Find someone, settle down, you'll be happier.'"

"Marriage today is not such a big thing as it was," explained the jogger philosophically. "Look at The New York Times. They're all marrying in their thirties after running corporations; then they get tired and want to be artificially inseminated. It's a gamble. Maybe it works, maybe not."

"We did things the natural way." The man nodded.

"And who says natural is better?" noted a tiny woman in a visor who had been waiting impatiently for a chance to enter the conversation. She had a reputation for stirring things up.

"Natural is nature. Nature is better," spelled out the man.

"You're not saying anything," said the woman with the visor. "You're speaking in circles."

"You're the one with circles," noted the man angrily. "Your brain"—he made a circle with his fingers to indicate a round, empty space—"is a circle."

"Do you have a boyfriend?" asked the jogger, turning to Amy in an effort to cut short what seemed to be escalating into a nasty confrontation. Amy indicated George. The group paused and contemplated this a moment. [George is Black.]

"Modern," said the man doubtfully. But after George had said a few words and been judged "not one of the angry ones," there was a palpable warming of opinion toward him.

"He's a nice boy," the jogger whispered to Amy. "Maybe he'll convert."

"And who's to say he's not Jewish?" said the man in the pink shorts. "There are Ethiopian Jews, you know."

I remember how, in writing this passage, I suddenly understood how to concoct the dialogue. Both the words spoken by the characters and the descriptive insertions had to have a certain musicality—a patter. This isn't real conversation; it's "shtick": a scene written for effect and, specifically, for laughs (the word is

Yiddish and so has an innate connection to early American vaudeville, where many of the performers were Jewish immigrants). Shtick is in keeping with this particular novel's broad comic conception, but it also seems to me that the rendering of any dialogue, if it is to be entertaining on the page—or in any medium for that matter where the observer is not inside it as a participant—must be a version of shtick; in other words, carefully edited for verve and interest, reflecting the idiosyncratic style of the author as she works to deliver a particular vision of life through writing.

When my daughter was growing up, we watched the show *Gilmore Girls* together, and I was taken with the highly articulate and probing conversations of the characters, Rory and Alexis, mother and daughter. They spoke with precision, intensity, and wit. "Let's talk like Rory and Alexis," I said to my daughter who, at fourteen or fifteen, merely rolled her eyes and walked away. In fact, talk between mother and daughter in the manner of *Gilmore Girls* is not possible, short of engaging in playacting, which defeats the purpose. Its characters relay a sense of structure and order, impossible in real life but that is enormously comforting and entertaining as the representation of real life.

We are surrounded by conversation of this sort (though generally not as good as in *Gilmore Girls*). We have chitchat on morning news and ongoing talk on twenty-four-hour cable news. We have jokey talk shows and earnest talk shows. Most either are trivial and cheery or hew obsessively to a party line (an exception is *Real Time with Bill Maher*, refreshing for its willingness to host guests across the aisle from each other and because Maher himself, though left-leaning, can be eclectic in his views). Most current talk shows on cable have niche audiences and are promotional ventures for guests who have just put out a new movie or TV series (rarely a book), forums for feel-good features, or exposés of scandal. The talk shows of yesteryear (Jack Paar, Dick Cavett, and even Johnny Carson) were better at providing substantively amusing or informative talk. Between 1965 and 1980, Carson's show lasted ninety minutes—a very long time—and he would interview authors in the last half hour, resulting in some memorable conversation. Cavett featured entertaining, ostensibly "high-brow" conversation, most memorably the erudite but venomous spat between Gore Vidal and Norman Mailer in 1971. Not polite but good television. William F. Buckley's *Firing Line* also aroused a certain morbid fascination for his prissy, elitist talk with guests who had opposing, liberal viewpoints. Until recently, *Charlie Rose* featured substantive talk until the show was cancelled for the misdeeds of its host.

Certain programs have the advantage of dealing with a specific subject area and thus can relay a more focused, analytical approach. *Inside the Actors Studio* and the French book discussion show *Apostrophe* are examples (both sadly defunct). Although not much of a sports enthusiast, I like the expertise on display in shows like *Inside NFL* and *Inside the NBA* where ex-players parse a game with the same laser precision with which literary scholars analyze *Paradise Lost*.

Some may argue that the demise of good talk on television is the fault of political correctness or (if one prefers another phrasing) ideological conformity, and though I think that a new vigilance about language can have a chilling effect on conversation, the real culprit, it seems to me, is anti-intellectualism and a curtailed attention span, the result of our social-media-saturated culture. Podcasts, which have gained steadily in popularity, are a kind of return to radio—accessed any time and allowing anyone to "perform," resulting in some lively, unsifted, conversation. Podcasts tend to be extremely niche-oriented, though they have the advantage, if not tethered to a network or advertisers, to be free of censorship or constraint and can therefore feel very close to eavesdropping on a genuine, live conversation.

As someone who has hosted a television interview show out of my university for more than fifteen years, I am aware of both the possibilities and pitfalls of talk as entertainment. The best interviews have an element of dramatic flamboyance about them that you wouldn't want in a private conversation. For example, my interview with author and director Nora Ephron about a year before her death had her trotting out material that I had read or heard many times before (her mother's edict, for example, that "everything is copy"), until we arrived at my question: "Don't you think that there are some good things about getting older?" Ephron paused, glared at me, and then gave a curt response: "No, nothing!" Retrospectively, I realized that she was thinking about her cancer diagnosis that no one at that point knew about. If this were a private conversation, it would have been a bad moment, but for an interview, it was dramatic and hence entertaining.

In a different but related example, I interviewed the actor Wendell Pierce (*The Wire, Treme*) about the devastation caused by Hurricane Katrina to his hometown of New Orleans. Thinking about this and about his grandmother, he began to cry at the end of the interview. It was as moving a moment as one could wish, the perfect coda to our taped conversation. Later, however, it occurred to me that perhaps that ending was too perfect. I wondered if the timing of those tears was related to Pierce's statement earlier in the interview about the importance of training very intensively for one's craft. As a consummate actor, was he channeling some of his Julliard education into our interview?

Some of my best interviews had moments that involved the click of a good rapport with someone. I felt this with the winner of the Man Booker Prize (Britain's highest literary award) John Banville; education expert Diane Ravitch; *New Yorker* writer Adam Gopnik; Michael Jackson biographer Margo Jefferson; and the late *Wall Street Journal* theater critic Terry Teachout. All five seemed to have an unquenchable love of ideas. I could imagine having more or less the same sort of conversation with them in private that I had for the camera, with the difference that I wouldn't feel obliged to cover requisite points and could have lingered longer on certain topics in which we had a shared interest.

· There were people I interviewed who exuded exceptional warmth and goodwill, and this spilled over into the formal setting of the interview: Karen Armstrong, the historian of religion, and the late biologist E. O. Wilson had this quality. I was drawn to journalist Bari Weiss because of the way she interacted with the students who were filming her episode (she seemed to be genuinely interested in their backgrounds and future plans). I found both Christopher Hitchens (also interviewed less than a year before his death) and Salman Rushdie to be especially fun to interview. I expected them to have canned answers, but they seemed spontaneous (unless of course they were so expert at interviewing as to *seem* spontaneous). The best interviewees had a sense humor that included the ability to laugh at themselves. Filmmaker John Waters, unsurprisingly, had that gift; he was pleased to describe the eyeliner he used to keep his signature pencil mustache intact.

The unscripted interview is perhaps the closest we can come to the enactment of conversation as it exists in private, though it is, by definition, one-sided. Movies and TV shows, in being scripted, are already far removed from the "flow" of conversation. In many movies, the talk between and among characters serves only to drive the action forward. In *The Maltese Falcon*, when the characters played by Sydney Greenstreet and Humphrey Bogart say they "like to talk," the statement seems an ironic commentary on their phlegmatic cat-and-mouse interaction; it bears no resemblance to the undirected back-and-forth that constitutes good talk.

There are exceptions, as with *My Dinner with André*, where the movie seems designed to give us insight into the dynamics of conversation. That film was directed by French director Louis Malle, and there's no doubt that the French seem able to represent substantive talk better than Americans. They've had more practice with it, and have more patience for watching it. The films of Eric Rohmer, in particular, have the wonderful capacity to make one feel that the characters are plumbing the depths of an idea. The 1969 film *Ma Nuit Chez Maud* always impressed me for its languorous drama (not an oxymoron) as it followed the trajectory of the talk between the two main characters, played by Jean-Louis Trintignant and Francoise Fabien, on the subject of religion and sex, late into the night.

On stage, the plays of Jean-Baptiste Poquelin, known as Molière, have the virtue of not veering away from conversation. Molière has been labeled the French Shakespeare, but what most distinguishes him from the great English playwright is where the drama of his work resides. In Shakespeare, there is character-driven action; in Molière, character-driven talk. This is in keeping with my view of French culture as deeply committed to thought and its expression in conversation. In Shakespeare, dramatic talk is mostly confined to the soliloquy— the conversation of the character with him- or herself—very different from the socially engaged conversation that occurs in Molière. (Shakespeare does give us the clever back-and-forth of

Beatrice and Benedick in *Much Ado about Nothing* and of Rosalind and Orlando in *As You Like It*, but this is banter, which Jonathan Swift said shouldn't count as conversation.)

Molière's most famous play, *The Misanthrope*, features a series of conversations between Philinte, a diplomatic courtier, and Alceste, who has no use for the politesse and conventions of court society. These two men are friends, and their conversations together are interspersed with Alceste's clashes with various other characters of the most preening, hypocritical sort. This includes the coquettish Celimène, an expert in social manipulation and duplicity, whom he loves against his will and better judgment.

Philinte accepts a world in which people lie and manipulate ("c'est normal"); Alceste vehemently rejects such a world. Here is an example of their positions (the translation is by poet Richard Wilbur, who captures the cadence and rhyme of Molière's verse):

> Philinte: When someone greets us with a show of
>   pleasure,
>   It's but polite to give him equal measure,
>   Return his love the best that we know how,
>   And trade him offer for offer, vow for vow.
> Alceste: No, no, this formula you'd have me follow,
>   However fashionable, is false and hollow,
>   And I despise the frenzied operations
>   Of all these barterers of protestations . . .

This dialogue between the accommodating diplomat and the extreme moral zealot structures the play and gives it its anchorage and wit. It is the kind of binary idea that the French enjoy elaborating on in conversation.

But Molière's *The Misanthrope* also reveals a basic fact about conversation as entertainment. It helps if it's complementary, even to the point of competition or combativeness. The clash of viewpoints is useful for both the drama and the humor of the play. Even on such rather predictable talk shows as *The View* or *The Talk*, the group recruited to discuss current events is deliberately chosen to represent different ideological positions. This allows debate and dispute and, for good television, an occasional blow-up. As I have already noted, many of the shows that currently dominate cable news programming present only one, uninflected viewpoint and therefore tend to grow stale and boring very quickly (at least for me).

I see the origins of conversation as entertainment emerging from late nineteenth-century American vaudeville and British music hall performance. Both of these forms of live entertainment featured a variety of "acts"—juggling, acrobatics, dance, instrumental and vocal performance, and comedy, either physical pratfall or verbal patter. Verbal patter (now called stand-up) was a kind of conversation with the audience (the comic supplies the jokes; the audience, the laughter or the hoots, boos, and occasional heckling). In some cases, comedy involved two characters in dialogue, to which the audience was both spectator and indirect participant.

The characters who made up these comic duos or doubles acts, as they are called, were, like Philinte and Alceste in Molière's play, complementary types: straight man and stooge (or funny man); sober judge and cut-up; cool guy and dweeb. Well-known examples (limiting myself to America) include George Burns and Gracie Allen, Dean Martin and Jerry Lewis, Bud Abbott and Lou Costello, Bing Crosby and Bob Hope, the Smothers Brothers, and Dan Rowan and Dick Martin. Jerry

Seinfeld, analyzing these pairs, has noted that the straight man looks at the stooge, but the stooge looks at the audience as though incorporating it into his foolishness.

These comedy duos that began in vaudeville moved to radio and film and, eventually, to television in the mid-twentieth century. The modeling of a kind of squabble between these characters was recognizable as an exaggeration of the kind of frustration we sometimes experience when trying to converse with intimates. In the case of George Burns and Gracie Allen, their actual marriage gave their act more point. As feminists, we may cringe at these closing lines (not actually said, I'm told, but often cited as emblematic of their interaction):

GEORGE: Say good night, Gracie.
GRACIE: Good night, Gracie.

But it's hard not to laugh. George's continual avuncular attempt to get Gracie to understand and her dogged ability to misdirect and literalize became a kind of congenial battle of the sexes—of deadpan versus whimsy, rationality versus instinct. It is, quite simply, delightful, since George never really got angry at Gracie, and Gracie always managed to relay some kind of sense in her zany rebuttals. I am tempted to say that she represented a guerrilla attack on patriarchy in her dogged unwillingness to understand in the terms that George intended.

The partners in the male comic duos incorporated the same stereotypical gender roles and, in the process, implicitly critiqued them. The stoical straight man occupied the stereotypical male role; the more helpless and gibbering stooge the stereotypical female one, suggesting that comic conversation relies on such complementarity but also deconstructs it. As with Burns and Allen, the serious, seemingly competent masculine type is often shown to be more of a fool than his flibber-tigibbet partner. This dynamic is carried through in buddy movies where the familiar back-and-forth is often punctuated by the karate-chopping of bad guys.

An interesting example of comic conversation at its most entertaining is the famous "Who's on First?" exchange between Abbott and Costello. Here's a snippet from that farcical exchange:

ABBOTT: Well, let's see, we have on the bags, Who's on first, What's on second, I Don't Know is on third. . . .

COSTELLO: That's what I want to find out.

ABBOTT: I say Who's on first, What's on second, I Don't Know's on third.

COSTELLO: Are you the manager?

ABBOTT: Yes.

COSTELLO: You gonna be the coach too?

ABBOTT: Yes.

COSTELLO: And you don't know the fellows' names?

ABBOTT: Well I should.

COSTELLO: Well then who's on first?

ABBOTT: Yes.

COSTELLO: I mean the fellow's name.

ABBOTT: Who.

COSTELLO: The guy on first.

ABBOTT: Who.

COSTELLO: The first baseman.

ABBOTT: Who.

And so on. . . . What most accounts for the delightful nature of this back-and-forth is the timing and delivery. Note that Abbott, the straight man, comes across as the reasonable figure; Costello as the dopey and uncomprehending one. But when we think about it for a moment, we see that Abbott's assumption that these names for the players are logical is itself absurd. It is a setup for farcical misunderstanding, not actually clever in the way of wordplay, only in the way of performance: the quickness and mugging with which this exchange plays out, Costello tying himself into knots as they proceed.

Abbott and Costello certainly practiced "Who's on First?" dozens, perhaps hundreds, of times so that they could perform it perfectly at breakneck speed. This is where the act most corresponds to real conversation of the best sort. While good conversation can be fast or slow—often alternating between these speeds—the nonstop nature of the vaudeville routine is a symbolic representation of "flow"—achieved in this case through exhaustive scripting and practice. It's what happens spontaneously between or among people when a conversation works.

The compressed hilarity of such comic duos gets transferred to the screen in the screwball comedies of the thirties and forties. For repartee, one cannot do better than watching Preston Sturges's characters' rapid-fire conversation or the back-and-forth between Katharine Hepburn and Spencer Tracy in their films together. On television, *The Honeymooners* features the same sort of complementary talk carried into the 1950s as Ralph Kramden starts out bombastically lecturing his wife Alice, and she ends by putting him definitively in his place.

The heirs to this kind of talk were popular sitcoms like *Cheers, Friends, Seinfeld*, and *Frasier* that featured fast-paced conversation, full of banter and fun. More recent long-form TV like *The Wire, Breaking Bad, The Sopranos, Ozark, True Detective, Big Little Lies*, and *The Good Place* contain more textured and in-depth conversation, given that they extend their narratives over multiple episodes. These shows require a considerable investment of time and attention to watch to the end, but this creates a shared sense of expectation as friends watch together and discuss the show. One could argue that long-form television has become a shared canon in an age in which most people no longer read the same books. It provides us with new, relatively substantive material to talk about.

CHAPTER 9

Conversation on Campus

When I was in sixth grade, I sat at a little desk in a designated row, filling out worksheets. I have no recollection of who sat next to me and what those worksheets were about; I only remember daydreaming about what I would eat for lunch. When I arrived in college, I spent my freshman year sitting in a large lecture hall with a group of anonymous students, staring at projected slides and daydreaming about lunch. In other words, not much had changed.

As my college career progressed, however, I was able to enroll in seminars and leave those deadly lectures behind. I know that some people enjoy lectures where they can sit passively in their chair and receive a warm bath of knowledge—but I am not one of them. I can learn only when I can actively participate. In a seminar, students must be "present." They usually sit in a circle and, ideally, around a table. The traditional term is a Harkness Table, derived from the 1930 gift of philanthropist Edward Harkness to the then all-boys preparatory school Phillips Exeter Academy. Harkness explained what he had in mind: a classroom where students "could sit around a table with a teacher who would talk with them and instruct them by a sort of tutorial or conference method, where [each student] would feel encouraged to speak up. This would be a real revolution in methods."

"A revolution in methods"—but of the simplest kind. The seminar replaces the lecturing of the professor in a large room with lively discussion in a small one. At least, that's the idea. Not all professors can inspire conversation with and among their students, and not all students are willing or able, even with the most adept prodding, to find something to say. But the goal of a seminar is to instigate talk that not only addresses the subject matter of the course but deepens and enlarges an understanding of it.

It is an obvious truism, codified by educators like John Dewey, that taking an active part in learning will help students understand the information better than being a passive recipient of it. But I would extend this further and say that a seminar course, where students can engage with each other about ideas, will teach them to become more adept conversationalists and, as a result, enjoy the verbal company of others in a way that will enrich their lives in the future and make them more engaged citizens.

Admittedly, a seminar can be daunting. Students are exposed; their verbal capacity and their ideas are more easily compared to those of their peers. The presence of the teacher can create an atmosphere of judgment that can be inhibiting and even frightening. During my own years in college, I sat in seminars where I could feel my breakfast turning over in my stomach as I tried to prepare a comment that would look both relevant and smart. I used to tally up how many times I managed to speak in my seminar classes on a given day. An attitude of this sort, fueled by anxiety and competitiveness, can create excitement and alertness, but it can also be debilitating. I don't see it as the best attitude to bring to a learning experience.

What one ideally wants from a seminar is that it be a place of welcome (in current parlance, a "safe space") as well as a spur to curiosity, attentiveness, and the expression of ideas. This is where seminar instructors become so important. They are the impresarios of the classroom and must find a way to make everyone feel accepted and engaged. If done well, this can seem effortless: knowing when to insert a comment, when to call on a reticent student, and when to remain entirely silent. Some teachers grasp this immediately; some take years to learn it; some never do. There is no formula for good seminar teaching, but one knows it when it happens—both as an instructor and a student. In a series of "Remembrances" of the Yale professor of classics and history Donald Kagan, his former students testified to his unerring ability to make a seminar work: "The conversation never felt like it was too regimented or, as frequently happens in seminars, aimless"; "he balanced his mental map with a willingness to explore interesting byways and tangents as they arose"; "he always stepped back and let the students run the class, guiding us from the sidelines, and intervening only when necessary. It was mysterious but it worked."

A good teacher is, in effect, a good conversationalist who has something particular to discuss (the subject matter of the course) but knows that remaining too closely tied to that subject matter will not only stifle the discussion but also inhibit the learning process. A seminar is a unique case of a conversation that is at once a means to an end (learning something) and an end in itself (engaging in the flow of group talk, where the personalities, back stories, and knowledge of each member of the class get a chance to be highlighted and appreciated).

Of the many seminars that I ended up taking in college, all of which were more memorable than the lecture classes that did not hold my attention, one in particular impressed itself indel-

ibly on my mind and heart. It was a junior seminar for majors
that surveyed English literature from Chaucer to T. S. Eliot.
There were about twelve of us in the class, meeting in a small
windowless room with a worn wooden table. The professor
did not have tenure (and would not get it at this institution),
and he was teaching material that was outside his field (he was
a medievalist, and this was a wide-ranging literature survey
with nothing from his period of specialization). But he was a
gifted professor with a love of books, and he worked hard to
make the seminar into a welcoming space for the exchange
of ideas.

I was always eager to go to that class. I never knew what my
classmates would say about what we had read, but I also never
knew what I would say, how I would insert myself into the discussion, what idea would pop into my head. But I never felt
inhibited or ashamed of my opinions. The professor had the gift
of making us all feel we had something to contribute that surprised and delighted him. He never passed judgment on our
insights except to say that they were insightful. Shame is the
great inhibitor of learning—and of conversation—and he eliminated it as an obstacle.

The novels and poems we read over the course of that term
became touchstones for me in later life. I retained many of the
theories put forward by my peers and by the professor (he would
occasionally trot out some of the theoretical ideas that were then
in vogue). That class spurred me to go on to study English literature in graduate school and became my model for how to teach.
More than forty years later I am still aspiring to create the kind of
excitement in the classroom that I felt then.

There are so many variables, large and small, that contribute
to the success of a seminar class: the subject matter, the teacher,
the mix of students, even the comfort of the chairs, the view out

the window, and the temperature in the classroom. There is undoubtedly an element of serendipity involved in whether these variables are present in the right form and combination, though an instructor can do a lot to mitigate the negatives when things are less than ideal. Still, there is only so much one can do, and sometimes a class just doesn't click.

Despite the many years I've taught, I am able to have true success in a seminar—where there is a delightful flow of conversation as it relates to and diverges from the subject matter—only in one of every five or six classes that I teach. When a seminar does work, however, the excitement and affection that result are palpable. I find myself learning along with the students, who continually surprise me with original insights. When the term is over, everyone in the class understands that something rare and mysterious has occurred and that our perspective on the world has been subtly but indelibly altered.

I tell students that one of the major goals they should have during their college years is to seek out classes and situations where they can learn to talk well about ideas, opinions, and feelings. A college seminar is a practice space for this—and, as such, for life. It requires that students learn how to deal with new material, listen attentively, and respond well to others' ideas, including how to civilly disagree, formulate, and articulate their own position. Along with these mundane benefits are spiritual ones: a seminar can lead to a mysterious kind of communion, where those present temporarily lose themselves in the material and in the wonder of each other's minds.

One of the criticisms that students of color have made about elite universities is that they aren't welcoming—that although they have been admitted to the college and sit beside white students in seminars, it is not easy for them to participate. I have to say that I felt the same when I was one of the few female students admitted to a formerly all-male college fifty years ago. I didn't think there was outright prejudice leveled against me (though no doubt that was there), but I rarely felt that anyone was making an effort to hear my opinion or help me engage (the exception was the literature course that I mentioned above).

Some will say that it is the job of the professor to make the classroom challenging, not welcoming. But those aspects of the classroom should not be at odds. Some students are not accustomed to a certain kind of discourse, and it is the professor's job to acclimate them—to help bridge the gap between those who have spent years in elite prep schools around Harkness Tables and those who have attended large public high schools in overcrowded classrooms where conversation is all but impossible. Those who have attended the latter may be no less intelligent than those in the former, but they need time and encouragement to learn how to verbally engage. As with so much else in life, conversation requires some degree of practice. The more one does it, the better one gets and the more pleasurable and satisfying it becomes. A professor who is attuned to this and makes the effort to create a climate of welcome, where those who speak up don't feel awkward or stupid, can change the whole tenor of a student's college experience.

Ideally, a seminar should flow from the classroom into the cafeteria or coffee shop. It should spur more thought and conversation: enthusiastic sharing and debate leading to camaraderie. This was certainly true for me with respect to that memorable seminar in college. My education proceeded into the dining hall and the library and, later, in my dorm room and the all-night diner where I still recall the taste of the hot tuna grinder that I consumed at two in the morning. I conversed with my peers not just about what I had read in class but on topics like whether God exists, whether there is such a thing as truth, and where to get the city's best pizza. That seminar taught me how to talk about subject matters both high and low, and find pleasure in the process.

Students are hungry for conversation of this sort, and even the least sophisticated have a dim sense that this is what college should be about.

Unfortunately, one can become habituated to not conversing much as one can become habituated to conversing. To me there are two impediments to conversation in the current college experience that parallel the class divide in our country. The first has to do with the nature of college for those with limited incomes. The kind of university that I am describing above—that many people I know attended—was a privileged space and a competitive and expensive one, even when I went there, though now, more so. Even with financial aid, some students are obliged to work in order to buy food and books, or to send money home to family members. In other cases, working students or those with children must attend community college at night or sandwiched between jobs and chores. In those cases, leisure is nonexistent, and the aim is to get a degree that will improve one's economic life rather than engage in the sort of desultory, exploratory conversation that I believe should be central to the college experience. I understand this and can see how, for these students, my argument may seem impractical and self-indulgent. Yet it is precisely the nonutilitarian and leisurely nature of conversation that makes it so valuable as a humanizing activity, a means by which we learn complex truths about ourselves and other people. I tell my students who work that they should choose their courses with care and take advantage of the opportunity to engage in conversation in the classroom, even if they have little time to do so outside of it.

The second group of students that seem to me to have suffered the loss of conversation are of the opposite sort: those privileged enough to be housed and fed on the campus and to spend their four years in what is often a highly protected, bucolic setting. Here, the impediment to conversation that has become ingrained in university life in the past thirty-five years or so is excessive drinking. I attribute the emergence of the college drinking culture to the raised legal drinking age, from eighteen to twenty-one, in 1984. When I was in college in the 1970s, alcohol was legal for eighteen-year-olds and was therefore present on campus but not abused in great quantities (with the exception perhaps of beer at football games). When the drinking age was raised, campus life changed. Making something forbidden tends to make it more enticing, especially among adolescents. Getting drunk has now become a goal, whereas before drinking was a means to more convivial interaction. As a preferred leisure activity, it is flagrantly and dangerously anti-intellectual, not to mention dangerous, pure and simple.

Both of the above impediments to conversation reflect problems in our society that we need to attend to. If we stress the importance of a college education, it is incumbent on us to think deeply about why it is important—how it differs from an apprenticeship or a technical education, even if the technical aspect is of the highest, most complicated sort. What should make college special is that it offers *time* during which students can explore ideas and learn about themselves and each other. Without the luxury of time and the desire to use it to converse, they are cheated of a valuable resource, no matter how illustrious their professors, how impressive the technical skills they acquire, or how high-paying the jobs they land after graduation.

It is worth considering why the time to converse is so valuable, and why college administrators should make it their business to foster an atmosphere conducive to talk.

For one thing, students in their late teens and early twenties are especially open to ideas. They are straddling the divide between childhood and adulthood, innocence and experience, and they are eager for connection and meaning. Their search for a soul mate supports this quest, and hence allows them to be more curious about and attentive to others.

Second is because college offers students material for conversation that will never again be as varied and wide-ranging. After graduation, they will need to focus on professional goals and devote themselves to narrower domestic matters.

Finally, college is one time in a person's life when there is the opportunity to easily meet people of different backgrounds and interests. Difference is a great fuel for conversation. Ideally, the world at large offers this diversity, and happily, our society is becoming more open to the diversity of race, gender, and ethnicity. But professional life tends to limit itself to like-minded people, if only because engineers generally work with engineers, graphic artists with graphic artists. College is designed to mix people with unlike interests together in student housing and classrooms. This is a spur to creative thinking and good conversation. But without the freedom from anxiety about money and career, much of what constitutes the best part of the college experience is lost.

I worry, moreover, not only about the expense of college and the incursions made by a campus drinking culture, but about the isolation that social media encourages and keeps young people on their phones and computers when they should be engaging with each other. There is an addictive quality to social media as much as there is to alcohol. Students have confessed to me that they sometimes feel driven to leave in the middle of a class to check their Facebook or Instagram page or respond to a text message. The immediate gratification that these forms of communication encourage is hard to resist; this makes in-depth, in-person conversation, which requires sustained, uninterrupted attention, difficult.

There is also the threat of grouptalk that I mentioned in chapter 4. I see this happening when a professor or an assemblage of students have an ideological viewpoint that they preach forcefully and without inflection. Students who don't feel as strongly or aren't as articulate go unheard. Not only are they left out of the discussion, but the opportunity for all present to hear another side of the issue is lost.

When the subject of discussion involves social justice, the problem is amplified. Who can disagree with acknowledging the wrongs of the past? Who would argue with the idea that injustice still lurks in our institutions and in the unexamined behavior of even well-meaning people? But how to address these problems is not simple. At times, the language used by idealistic students and even faculty is sloppy and generalized, making talk a kind of rote repetition of virtuous ideas. Often, it's not a matter of agreeing or disagreeing with the ideas so much as taking issue with the dogmatic style in which they are presented.

Good conversation digs deep into a subject, turns it over, examines it from angles that might otherwise remain in shadow, and presents hypotheses that may be wrong or even unpleasant, but thought-provoking. When there is no tolerance for wrong or unpleasant, the result can be conformist and platitudinous. I used to routinely adopt the devil's advocate position in class as a means of complicating what was being discussed, but I find it harder to do this now, when dissenting viewpoints are less tolerated and when playful or ironic positions are taken literally.

Several well-known comedians have announced that they will no longer perform on college campuses because they feel inhibited by what they can make jokes about. Humor is, by definition, disruptive and even offensive. Conversation, while it need not be offensive, ought nonetheless to push the boundaries of the already known and accepted.

In a climate of ideological rigidity, it can be difficult to get students to share their views, but good teachers will make it their task to elicit what everyone really thinks, even if the result is messy; they will not pass judgment (unless the basic facts are wrong). Bad teachers will assume that there is a right answer and push it as incontrovertible, thereby blocking the flow of conversation. (I see activist teachers as bad teachers who should be doing community organizing rather than teaching.) In an atmosphere of welcome and safety, students who have been silent can be encouraged to express themselves and those who have stubbornly held to one, uninflected view can become more ready to listen and assimilate new ideas.

When students take an active part in a seminar they are far more likely to retain the material being discussed than if they are simply fed it in a lecture course. As Columbia professor Andrew Delbanco has argued, students who engage in seminar talk will also be better citizens; they will have the tools needed to evaluate and speak out against injustice and incompetence, and be better equipped to handle complex situations that arise after they graduate. And they will perform better in the workplace. This may not show itself immediately; entry-level jobs are notoriously limited in allowing for individual expression. But in time, those who have learned to talk in seminars know how to elicit ideas from others and have the ability to generalize and abstract—as well as to discriminate, argue, and listen well, skills that are valuable in any career.

I like to give the example of a friend who trained as an anthropologist and spent years in seminars, both as a student and as an instructor, but who eventually left academia for advertising and became an expert at running focus groups. Of everyone at his firm, he was best equipped to get a group of diverse individuals to give insights useful to a client. Other settings rely on people who have the ability to not only talk well but steer talk in a particular direction and inspire others to be creative and insightful—precisely what teachers and students do in seminar courses (when a seminar works, the students as well as the teacher are instigators of ideas and can, at times, assume a leadership role in the group). Government caucuses and committees, business task forces, workshops, and brainstorming sessions all require the ability to do this. Beyond such utilitarian ends, an adept conversationalist can help create an atmosphere of connectedness, goodwill, and joy that can improve the quality of the work environment.

The kind of conversation that I am describing as so important for success after graduation is mostly found in seminar courses in the humanities (and the increasingly less common qualitative social sciences). Unfortunately, the humanities are now endangered fields of study in universities, usurped by disciplines believed to guarantee more lucrative careers. Business and STEM fields rely heavily on technical skills and are often focused on solving isolated problems rather than exploring questions in context. They are not designed, at least on the undergraduate level, to encourage the kind of nuanced, critical thinking associated with literature, history, and philosophy and their offshoots, theater, art history, and media studies.

As already noted, the Russian critic Bakhtin has written about the "dialogic" nature of the novel form, concentrating on the work of Dostoevsky, which he describes as containing "a genuine polyphony of fully valid voices." I would argue in contradiction to Bakhtin, who sees this polyphony as unique to the novel genre, that other representational forms can incorporate "fully valid voices," if not in the same way: the plays of Shakespeare, the music of jazz groups, the long-form television series, multimedia art. Closely examining work of this kind opens students to indeterminacy, ambiguity, nuance, and contradiction, which are motors for conversation but also frameworks by which they can assess the meaning and importance of any pursuit. To want to save the planet is a desirable goal, but it requires that we define the environment and the place of the human within it.

While I am devoted to the humanities as the best possible spur to good conversation, I also believe that schooling in this area can lead to better conversation around STEM subject matter. There is a current movement to bring a more equitable perspective to the teaching of math and science, and the idea has received a good deal of ridicule and pushback. People wonder how equity can be relevant to the teaching of math. I believe it can. If we could teach math around a Harkness Table—focusing on seminar-style concepts rather than (or in addition to) the memorization of formulas—the discipline could be made more accessible and intellectually stimulating to a broader range of students. I would have liked to have had a math class in which a formula was carefully deconstructed. Perhaps two ways at solving a problem could be compared and discussed, with a focus on the kind of thought process that each engenders. This would open up the field, intellectually and creatively. If I look back on my math education, I see that it was rushed and rigidly organized: I was expected to do the requisite problem sets and then move on to the next step, going somewhere more important and difficult, instead of lingering on what I was learning and why. I managed to pass calculus, but I had no real understanding of what I was doing. I don't think I was alone in this. As a remedy, I hope to encourage experiments in a more leisurely style of thinking about math and science in the course offerings in the Honors College where I am dean if I can find instructors with the conceptual and pedagogical skills to take this on.

I cannot end a chapter about conversation on campus without addressing how important it is for faculty as well as students to engage with each other. This used to be the great draw of an academic career: one could converse with a wide variety of people who loved ideas and had devoted their lives to them in an environment conducive to collegial sharing. There was time for long lunches and summers off to do research and share new knowledge with interested peers.

But this aspect of university life has mostly disappeared. The atmosphere now is more competitive and more politically charged. Forty years ago, when I first arrived at my university, the faculty club offered three meals a day. On the same floor of the building was a cozy bar that opened at four o'clock and that a variety of faculty and staff, including the university president, frequented on a regular basis. My friend Dave liked to recall how he and the president, after a few drinks, cooked up the idea of making a documentary film about the introduction of microcomputers to the university (this was the early 1980s and the film was made—with a cameo from Steve Jobs, whose Macintosh was the computer the university had chosen to make available to all students). Back then, faculty members looked forward to collegial conversation, and new courses and research projects were hatched over meals or drinks.

By the early 1990s, the bar had closed and, long before the pandemic hit, the faculty club had long ceased to serve breakfast and dinner. Lunch was offered but was woefully attended.

People complained that the food was bad, but that wasn't the real problem. Faculty members weren't motivated to meet each other. They were focused on their own research and didn't want to take time away from busy schedules to trek a block or two to the club. Only one table was regularly occupied—by a group of septuagenarian engineers. These men (for they were all men) were lively conversationalists—and several of us, members of the English department, would occasionally join them. Their impresario was an electrical engineer who would expound, Dr. Johnson-like, on everything from opera to politics, the rest chiming in at intervals. It was the last remaining vestige of the collegial university of yesteryear.

In 1999 the American Association of University Professors put out a statement about the use of "collegiality" in tenure decisions: "The very real potential for a distinct criterion of 'collegiality' to cast a pall of stale uniformity places it in direct tension with the value of faculty diversity in all its contemporary manifestations." This viewpoint makes sense—the traditional focus on collegiality was sometimes a code for homogeneity, mediocrity, and support for the "old boy" network. But the combination of groupthink and careerism that has overtaken academia in recent years is another kind of blight. It's important to have a community of scholars who gather together and talk. If faculty do not practice conversation of the best sort among themselves, it is unlikely that they can bring these skills to bear in the classroom.

The problem resides in the decline of a culture that supports humanistic values and that, instead, sees the professor and student in terms of big data and bureaucratic goals rather than as unique individuals dedicated to the life of the mind and the free play of ideas. If that can be resurrected, then collegiality will take care of itself.

There exists a field of study called conversation theory that uses cybernetics to connect various disciplines through iterative forms of exchange. The focus is on artificial intelligence and machine learning as an adjunct to traditional instruction, which seems very far from the kind of loose and open conversation that I see as valuable in helping students connect with each other and learn (two functions that go hand in hand). Still, the idea of change as the result of feedback, which is the premise of cybernetics, is central to conversation. It is possible that artificial intelligence can help model some aspects of this for us. The university should be the place where this research is carried out, but it is hoped that some of the lessons can be applied to human rather than simply machine processes.

CHAPTER 10

Shakespeare on Zoom

The COVID-19 pandemic limited our interactions with each other, and most of us are delighted to see this period of deprivation and isolation wane. As someone devoted to conversation, I value the serendipitous meeting—running into a friend, colleague, or student and taking time to sit on a bench or grab a coffee together. This was one of the pleasures of living in a walkable city and working on a college campus: you never knew whom you might meet and where that might lead.

The pandemic did away with this sort of experience. It overlaid the already increased physical isolation that social media has wrought with the fear of contagion.

Online learning has long been available to those who cannot afford or find time to attend a university in person. But the pandemic has created a new kind of integration of online learning into the standard university curriculum. This has raised a host of new questions. To what extent should the university cater to remote students? Should courses at so-called traditional universities be all face-to-face, hybrid (partially online), or hyflex (simultaneously online and face-to-face)? I worry about how the answers to these questions will affect the integrity of higher education when undergraduate experience already supports what I see as overly compartmentalized learning, as I discussed in the previous chapter.

I feel strongly about the dangers of becoming too acclimated to life online. Several recent books have testified to the importance of "touch"—which is, at least potentially, possible when one sees people in person (albeit less so now within a culture more attuned to harassment issues). But even without touch, the fact of real bodies in the presence of each other seems to me important. When the body is consistently reduced to two dimensions, what is likely to result? The relationship between dysmorphic body issues and virtual reality has not been sufficiently studied, though some commentators have raised the issue.

Yet there are also positive elements attached to the online experience that deserve attention and support. COVID-19 has made us aware of situations where Zoom can make possible conversations that would otherwise be impossible. (How these positive aspects should be integrated into the college experience is, as I noted, difficult to say.)

Let me begin by summarizing the three most obvious benefits of face-to-face interaction and follow with their parallel benefits online.

First, on behalf of face-to-face:

1. We see the whole person and can read people's body language as well as hear their words.
2. We can interrupt and speak over others with animation (what Deborah Tannen calls "cooperative overlapping"), creating a more spirited encounter.
3. We can continue the engagement after the class or meeting is over, recessing to lunch or coffee, making new friends and developing new ideas as a consequence.

Recontextualizing the above points, here are the benefits of conversing on Zoom:

1. We can see others' faces in close-up in their own space with no bodily or contextual distractions.
2. We cannot interrupt, but must wait to unmute before speaking, which can create a more mannerly and equal exchange.
3. We can exist at a distance from each other and need not travel to come together.

I would add to the above three dualities, one associated with self-presentation. I know many people who welcomed the ease of holding meetings in their pajamas (the bottoms, at least). But there are others, of which I count myself one, who missed the pleasures of getting dressed—of the clothes and accessories involved in presenting oneself to the world. This can seem like a trivial or an important pleasure, depending on your perspective (and may hinge on whether your mother conditioned you to like to go shopping for clothes).

I tip heavily in favor of in-person interaction (and not just because I like to get dressed). At the same time, I can attest to instances where conversing remotely offers exceptional benefits—benefits that we would never have realized were it not for the COVID-19 lockdown.

One such case involves older people. I know a club in my city that has long had difficulty recruiting members owing to how hard it is for some of the elderly, living in the suburbs or in support facilities, to make their way to a meeting. During the pandemic, the club's discussions went online. Now, as the pandemic ebbs, equipment has been purchased to make possible a hyflex delivery: those who can make the live meetings come for lunch and discussion; those who can't join remotely and can be seen and heard on a screen set up in the front of the room.

From my own experience, I can point to one instance in which meeting on Zoom has been spectacularly worthwhile. This is an online group that began early in the pandemic and is likely to continue indefinitely, no matter where we are or what we are doing elsewhere in our lives, something that an in-person group would never pretend to. I can imagine joining from a mountaintop or a hospital bed, ceasing to sign in only when I am either dead or comatose.

The reason for our gathering is to read Shakespeare. I call it a "Shakespeare Read Aloud," but it is much more than that and has come to contain all the ingredients of great, ongoing conversation. I would go so far as to compare it to the kind of conversation that Dr. Johnson and his friends famously engaged in at their London club.

My group had its origins before the pandemic, when I began meeting with three students in my office to read *Othello*. Other responsibilities interfered, and we disbanded before getting very far. After the pandemic began, I sent out a notice to resurrect the Shakespeare group. Four people, including two of the original students, initially joined. A week or so later, a few more people signed on: two staff members from the university, two English professor friends, and an alum who had seen the announcement in one of the university newsletters. We began by reading *As You Like It*, a play sure to lift our spirits during the plague year.

Some of those present had had extensive experience with Shakespeare and read with fluency and expressiveness; others had never read Shakespeare before and had to be told to watch the punctuation and not worry about stumbling over odd or archaic words. We moved very slowly, stopping whenever something was unclear to the group—or to me—and discussed this at whatever length was warranted.

Very soon, those present had invited several others who they thought would enjoy a careful reading experience of Shakespeare. There is a mystique to this playwright; he is understood to be great but also difficult. This can frighten some off but be alluring to others. To discover, as these people did, that Shakespeare *is* great but not actually that difficult is revelatory.

We gained and lost members over the first few months until we finally settled into a dozen. This group, with occasional stray add-ons, has remained stable ever since. The age range is considerable—from eighteen to seventy-eight—with backgrounds and levels of expertise that are just as divergent. There are now enough people so that we can have many voices included in our reading and analysis. I assign new parts as we move from scene to scene so that everyone has a chance to read, but we stop after each scene—and sometimes after only a few lines—to parse and comment. What makes this group unique is that it is not a course; there are no grades or assignments; it is a purely voluntary, entirely nonutilitarian gathering. I suspect that this is central to its success. We have fashioned a space where conversation happens without a goal in mind other than the pleasure afforded by great literature and the delight of being in the presence of other lively and interested minds.

In the course of our two years together, we have discussed a multitude of issues relating to Shakespeare: what he borrowed from earlier sources and what he did with it to make it inimitably his own; the nature of his genius and what constitutes genius. We have also teased out meaning that is relevant to our lives. These include political insights that dovetail with current events, and more personal and domestic ideas relating to occupation and gender issues as well as parental, sibling, filial, and romantic relationships.

As of this writing, we have read nine plays with a thoroughness that we all feel is exceptional. For me, it is as though we have wrung the plays dry with our penetrating and multiangled approach. It helps that we have young, progressive readers and older, more conservative ones. We have an ardent Catholic, a lapsed Catholic, a few Jews of variable piety, and a smattering of Protestants. We are white, Black, and East Asian. Most of us live in Philadelphia, but several are from out of state and one resides in England. We have some members who are exceptionally well educated; and others who have not yet finished college. But the feeling of the weekly reading is so convivial, so intellectually alive, and so safe that we look forward to this gathering as the high point of our week. I was the instigator and am the moderator; I have had perhaps the most experience with Shakespeare; but I do not feel like I am an expert or even a teacher so much as a coordinator. We are all equal in this congenial conversation about material that is deep, linguistically accomplished, clever, sometimes laugh-out-loud funny, and full of relevance to life both in general and to our own individual lives.

At one point during the summer, someone told a "Talk of the Town" writer at the *New Yorker* about our Read Aloud. He attended and watched from his little box for the entire hour as we read, stopped, analyzed, squabbled, digressed, laughed, and continued on. It was a glorious session, but he seemed only mildly interested. He gave us a friendly nod and was gone. No article ensued. I realized that to be an onlooker to what we did would not capture the feeling of participation. No doubt the reporter thought that any group reading and discussion would proceed like this. What he couldn't know was that we were all immersed in a feeling of unparalleled connectedness, intellectual excitement, and goodwill. But you would have had to be inside the conversation for a while to understand this.

We all pretty much feel the same way about the wonder of our group; we don't miss a week except for the direst emergency, and we often have to tear ourselves away when the hour is up and end the Zoom. While my university has returned to face-to-face teaching, it would not be feasible for our Shakespeare Read Aloud to meet in person, given the age and distance separating some of the participants. I would add that we have now become acclimated to the particularities of seeing each other online. We all comfortably reside in our little boxes and find it disorienting when, occasionally, we meet someone from the group in person.

As a group, we have come to appreciate Shakespeare's greatness—and often exclaim in praise of his depth and range. His work contains a multitude of perspectives because he gives all his characters, including his villains, a genuine voice. Shylock, for example, in *The Merchant of Venice*, supplies a counterpoint—a complicating perspective—to that of the other characters. He is an example of a character, conventionally silenced in the society depicted, whom Shakespeare allows to express the *cri de coeur* of the abused outsider, made villainous by the treatment he has suffered at the hands of the powerful and privileged:

> Hath
> not a Jew eyes? hath not a Jew hands, organs,
> dimensions, senses, affections, passions? fed with
> the same food, hurt with the same weapons, subject
> to the same diseases, healed by the same means,
> warmed and cooled by the same winter and summer,

as a Christian is? If you prick us, do we not bleed?
if you tickle us, do we not laugh? if you poison
us, do we not die? and if you wrong us, shall we not
revenge? If we are like you in the rest, we will
resemble you in that. If a Jew wrong a Christian,
what is his humility? Revenge. If a Christian
wrong a Jew, what should his sufferance be by
Christian example? Why, revenge. The villany you
teach me, I will execute, and it shall go hard but
I will better the instruction. (III, i)

The speech stops readers in their tracks and forces them to reassess everything they had thought about the play's heroes and
villains.

Once we "hear" Shylock's voice, we also hear additional resonance in the voices of more seemingly conventional characters,
Antonio and Portia, the gay man and the woman, whose marginality we might otherwise have overlooked. To this, we add
the voices of our reading group, each of us with a different perspective and set of experiences, each with our own subjectivity
(George Eliot refers to this in her great novel *Middlemarch* as
that "equivalent centre of self, where the lights and shadows
must always fall with a certain difference"). The unique perspective of each of us informs our interpretation of the characters' lines and hence complicates them in a multitude of sometimes contradictory ways.

Everyone in our Shakespeare Zoom now reads with a certain
amount of fluency, is able to trace recurring patterns and note
tics of style, and has theories about Shakespeare's philosophy
of life, his sexuality, and his moral sense. The plays are full of
interesting matter, but they are also in some sense secondary,
since they serve as the means of our communion. I cannot

imagine any other way that we could so gracefully and safely register our tastes, fears, and desires than through the medium of Shakespeare's great poetry and characterizations. As we move through each play, we learn about ourselves and each other alongside the characters whose words and actions we analyze. It is a profound and joyful symbiosis. I do believe that the feeling of love, which I mentioned early in this book as a hallmark of good conversation, has infused this group of readers and commentators. I see facets in these people that I know I would never have encountered had we not communed over the plays.

Shakespeare made this possible, but I imagine that any great work would serve in the same way: as a vehicle for insight and connectedness. In the case of Shakespeare, the richness and complexity of his words were the medium through which we found intellectual and emotional inspiration. Our Read Aloud kept us sane and, more than sane, kept joy and fellowship alive during the physical isolation and mental despondency of the pandemic. It continues to do this now that the period of quarantine is over and we continue to struggle with the challenges of living.

Conclusion

The saying, attributed to Spanish philosopher George Santayana, goes, "Those who do not remember the past are condemned to repeat it." This statement has power because we tend to see patterns in human life that, in retrospect, seem cautionary and suggest how we ought to have acted in the face of them. The problem with the statement is that it assumes that we can "remember" history with objective accuracy. Even when amended to refer to studying rather than remembering, the assumption remains that history is a monolithic block of information that we can learn if we spend enough time in a library carrel.

Given what I know from my relatively long life experience, I would alter the above statement into a clunkier form as follows: *Those who do not discuss different perspectives on history will not achieve the wisdom needed to be able to make good judgments in the present.*

Even if we read books about the past that present different perspectives, the reading, if done in isolation, can be filtered only through our own singular understanding of life. If, however, we converse with others alongside our reading, we gain the benefit of multiple viewpoints from different experiences and funds of knowledge as they interact vitally with our own.

I was reminded of this in reading the reviews of Stephen Greenblatt's Pulitzer Prize–winning book *The Swerve*. Greenblatt argues in that work that a nodal point in history was the rediscovery of *De Rerum Natura* (*On the Nature of Things*), a long, philosophical poem, written in the first century BCE by the Roman poet Lucretius. The poem had disappeared during the medieval period when classical learning, according to Greenblatt, was effectively erased by the Church. This Church-dominated period, he said, was, as traditional scholarship had dubbed it, "the Dark Ages." The resurfacing of Lucretius's poem, owing to the efforts of fifteenth-century Italian biblio-phile Poggio Bracciolini, brought a more expansive, humanis-tic vision back into circulation. Lucretius's work, which derives from the Epicurean philosophy that preceded him, presents a world that seems without a guiding intelligence or Godlike creator. It is made up of tiny particles (Lucretius's anticipation of atoms) that he argues were originally arranged in uniform fashion but, at some point, "swerved" to produce the complex-ity of the universe as we know it. The title of Greenblatt's book refers both to this swerve and to the swerve—or paradigm shift—that he postulates happened with the rediscovery of Lucretius's poem. He sees the vision of nature presented in the poem as the model for a modernity in which humanism and science prevail over the narrow, repressive vision he associates with the medieval church.

Greenblatt's view of history is supportive of a modern, secu-lar, science-oriented culture. His book is supremely readable, full of narrative twists and turns that carry the nonexpert reader along. I enjoyed it immensely and know many other people who did. But several reviewers have argued with Greenblatt on a number of fronts. One critic, for example, maintains that his representation of medieval culture is wrongheaded, another that his view of Lucretius is a serious misreading. Having read Greenblatt's book and many reviews of it, some critical, some laudatory, I find myself at an impasse as to what to believe. I suppose I could try to read Lucretius, which would have to be in translation, which itself constitutes an interpretation. It would be even harder for me to do a comprehensive historical study of the period that Greenblatt labels the Dark Ages but that others see as possessing much more of the grounding for modernity and thus more light than he seems to believe.

What I can do, however, is talk about the book with others—philosophers, historians, and otherwise serious readers who, together, have a breadth of diverse knowledge. How do they see the book? Do they agree with the praise it received? Do they feel that it talks down to them, as one reviewer argued; that it lacks seriousness and is too devoted to making itself into a best seller, as another states? Are some of these views, as one of my friends maintained, swipes by academics who distrust Greenblatt's success in crossing over from the scholarly to the popular (something that I can identify with, having tried to do the same)? The variety of "takes" strikes me as the stuff that makes for good conversation and, as a by-product, would help me place the book in a wider context of meaning. Indeed, if we use Greenblatt's book as the basis for a conversation, we would come to a better understanding of the slippery nature of historical interpretation. We would also learn more about what the people with whom we discuss the book find important and persuasive.

I have begun to have these conversations, and I can't say that I have arrived at any definitive conclusion about *The Swerve*. That may be the point. There are aspects to Greenblatt's book that I believe are persuasive; others that, especially in light of counterarguments, seem to me less so. I admire the book's readability while also seeing how this requires a certain reductiveness in the representation of ideas and historical events. My reservations throw me back upon myself. Is my wariness about the book's popularity a kind of snobbism? Being a writer myself, might I be driven by a certain competitiveness? I've found it useful to also turn these issues over with friends in conversation. There is a lot to examine in figuring out what I think and then to interrogate why I think it.

But I want to use Greenblatt's book for another purpose as well. *The Swerve* argues that Lucretius's poem sparked an intellectual revolution. The Greeks and Romans had a thriving humanistic society that went into eclipse during the medieval period and then resurfaced in the Renaissance. This death and resurrection of the human spirit of inquiry seems overly simplistic, as some critics have pointed out, but it does supply us with a model to think about when societies and cultures seemed to thrive and when they don't.

For I would like to borrow from Greenblatt the idea that, during the classical period, conversation was lauded as a value. For the Romans, in particular, the art of rhetoric was practiced, and friendship was highly prized—both spheres in which wide-ranging talk figures importantly. The medieval period, by contrast, focused attention around Christian subjects and the fate of the individual soul. Its favored literary forms were holy manuscripts and religious sermons; it valued the monastic life of silence and prayer. It was not an era in which conversation flourished, at least not in ways that the public at large could see and imitate. The Renaissance, beginning with the poet Petrarch, brought back the idea of conversation, though without abandoning the influence of Christianity, which now served to humanize rather than to distance it from mutual dialogue.

One can argue that only when conversation is free and flourishing does a society thrive in the ways that most of us value. The suppression of free speech is not just the suppression of public speech and of the media; it leads to a general unwillingness—

and eventually an inability—on the part of individuals to engage honestly and openly with each other in private. Hence, Franco's Spain, Hitler's Germany, and Stalin's Russia were suppressive of uninhibited, creative conversation. People began to automatically self-censor and hence either not speak together or speak in ways that slavishly duplicated the party line. (There was subversive, underground talk in all these regimes, to be sure, but those who engaged in it did so in fear for their lives. That can produce brilliance but not what Virginia Woolf referred to as the pleasures of "rational intercourse.")

Self-censorship eventually leads to a restriction in thought. If we return to Descartes's maxim, "I think, therefore I am," we see that to fail to think turns individuals into nonhuman automatons. In *The Origins of Totalitarianism*, Hannah Arendt, writing in the aftermath of Nazi Germany, argues that under a totalitarian regime, both those in power and those who are victimized lose an essential part of their humanity and are unable to think for themselves. They not only are prevented from conversing freely but lose a sense of what it means to do so. In other words, shared diversity of opinion makes us more human and our society more humane; its absence results in the opposite.

I would add to this my feeling that conversation is also a source of healing—a therapeutic good for the individual and the society. This returns me to Freud's talking cure. His notion of healing was clinical and confined to the individual psyche. Mine is social and involves mutuality. We give each other support when we engage with honesty and goodwill about subjects large and small. We assert our humanity and become more acutely aware of the humanity of others. This makes us better friends and neighbors and, as such, better citizens.

To make my point more emphatically, I turn again to the genre of the novel that, like Bakhtin, I find to be a good way to represent profound ideas that have not been stripped of their human indeterminacy. In this case, I refer to a character in Leo Tolstoy's *War and Peace* as an example of how conversation can salve our psychic needs as we move about in a contentious society.

Several years ago, I taught *War and Peace* to fourteen unusually engaged students and was more struck than I was on previous readings by the character of Pierre Bezukhov. He is the sleeper hero of the novel. The illegitimate son of an enormously wealthy count, he serendipitously inherits his father's enormous fortune. His new wealth and status both give him power and open him to exploitation. Aimless and without intimate connections, he wanders through the novel, suffering and seeking meaning. Pierre is described as stout and unprepossessing, foolish, mildly debauched, and absent-minded. He is one of a slew of characters that populate this novel, all with predictably confusing Russian names.

Students have compared Pierre to Waldo, the character in the illustrated children's book *Where's Waldo?*, whom you have to pick out in different crowd scenes. He is also a Zelig figure, popping up at highly dramatic and historically important moments in the novel: he marries the beautiful, socially adept (and mercenary) Helena; engages in a pistol duel in which he accidentally wounds a swaggering rival; is inducted into Freemasonry in an elaborately mystifying ceremony; is present during the bloody Battle of Borodino as Napoleon's troops approach Moscow; rescues a child from a burning building; is pardoned at zero hour as he is about to face a firing squad; and is imprisoned and led on a forced march until liberated by his Russian compatriots. All this allows Tolstoy to describe important moments in history from the perspective of someone who is not exceptionally talented or heroic—an everyman of sorts.

But Pierre is also a moral and emotional touchstone. Although my students barely registered him when he first made his appearance, they became increasingly attached to him as the novel progressed—precisely what Tolstoy must have had in mind. We often ignore or neglect the truly authentic people in our midst and glom onto the bravura types who dazzle us but have no real texture or depth.

Pierre is a conflicted figure for much of the novel. He struggles to make sense of his life and how he can make a contribution in the world. After his loveless marriage and the discovery of his wife's affair with a friend, he thinks he has found an answer in the high-flown ideals of Freemasonry, but is disappointed here too: "Even those members who seemed to be on his side," he concludes, "understood him in their own way with limitations and alterations he could not agree to, as what he always wanted most was to convey his thought to others just as he himself understood it." He continues his quest, only to see his city devastated and be witness to horrific cruelty at the hands of the Napoleonic invaders. Yet he ultimately emerges with a more generous and enlarged perspective. His experience and observation of suffering have healed him of the angst and uncertainty—and the need for agreement—that have gripped him throughout the novel. Tolstoy describes Pierre's new perspective as an "acknowledgment of the impossibility of changing a man's convictions by words, and his recognition of the possibility of everyone thinking, feeling, and seeing things each from his own point of view." But this recognition does not defeat him. On the contrary, he discovers another way forward.

I find Pierre's epiphany enormously profound and comforting. I have always believed in the saving power of words, and been disappointed again and again as words fail to solve the difficulties and divisions I see around me. Pierre's understanding that he can't use words to change other people's minds is revelatory. For though he gives up on the instrumental power of words, he does not give up on conversation. On the contrary, Pierre finds himself talking with others more than ever. His ability to listen, be curious, empathize, and share his own experiences makes him a magnet for the stories and confessions of those he encounters. He is no longer focused on finding points of agreement, winning arguments, or discovering the "right" path, but on accepting people in their difference and engaging with them where they are.

This seems to me a useful perspective—a way forward in our present moment. Now, when changing minds seems so difficult, we ought to speak to each other more than ever. Our attitude should be that people are not reduceable to their opinions—or, rather, they are more than what their stated opinions might simplistically lead us to believe.

The character of Pierre Bezukhov demonstrates how to take the long view on trivial quarrels—and most quarrels are trivial, if we back up far enough to see them clearly. Although the First Epilogue to the novel suggests that Pierre becomes something of an activist, attempting to help organize the peasants in support of a better life, his attitude is not rigid or angry, and he is able to discuss his ideas with the conservative Nikolay, whose relationship to the peasants remains traditionally patriarchal.

Pierre has found peace with what he cannot know and do. He is able to appreciate the love of his family and friends, and can engage with others in their complex humanity without having to change their minds. Tolstoy frames everything in a spiritual context—his Second Epilogue makes clear his larger theories about history and God—but we need not accept these to appreciate what Pierre achieves and to use it as a model for imitation. What he represents most of all is a state of mind that is alert and receptive without feeling that a definitive answer must be found. This is at the core of good conversation, that moves with no definitive point of rest or resolution, always open to the wonder of other minds and to the ways our own can surprise us.

Coda

Speech after long silence; it is right,
All other lovers being estranged or dead,
Unfriendly lamplight hid under its shade,
The curtains drawn upon unfriendly night,
That we descant and yet again descant
Upon the supreme theme of Art and Song:
Bodily decrepitude is wisdom; young
We loved each other and were ignorant.

This poem, written in 1932 by Irish poet William Butler Yeats, has always been among my favorites. But I have responded differently to it at different points in my life. It seemed clever to me when I was young, prophetic when I was middle-aged, and wistful and sad as I grew older. But as I have approached "bodily decrepitude," I have also come to see that the poem, beautiful though it is, is disturbingly reductive. I want to amend it to suit my current needs.

I can remember many instances in my youth of being led by desire and elevated hope. But I was also far from silent during these periods. It was through conversation that I got to know the people I came to love, who have sustained me over time. In this respect, the shift from action to talk, from love to wisdom that Yeats outlines in the poem doesn't seem right. We shift back and forth between these states at every period of our lives.

It's true that at the current place where I find myself certain activities are no longer possible or desired. I can't easily hike up a mountain and don't feel inclined to party all night or sky-dive (though a student of mine has tried to tempt me to do this). But the conversations I have with others continue to be full of life and vigor, capable of expressing love and friendship. I feel replenished, rejuvenated, and energized when I talk with people.

It seems to me a poem is a very solitary thing, and perhaps I am not made to take its solitary esthetic too seriously. I like the socially created world of conversation where we try to make things fun for each other, where we recast our experiences in a manner that will uplift rather than depress, and where we can forget ourselves—which includes forgetting the fact that we can't do everything we once did, that our options in life have narrowed, and that we are mortal. In conversation, at its best, all that fades to insignificance, even when it is the subject being discussed. If this is what Yeats means by "art and song," it is art and song shared in conversation with others and, in the process, renews our sense of life and love up until the end.

Bibliographical Essay

This book draws on my more than forty years of teaching, reading, writing, and, of course, conversing with people of all kinds. I've spent my career in a university setting but one that is unusually diverse and open to different forms of expression. I want to thank my students and my staff for keeping me grounded in the vital tumult of the world.

A number of works have been influential in all facets of my life, and thus in shaping my thoughts about conversation. One is the work of Sigmund Freud, from whom I take the title of this book. I see Freud as a cultural critic of great insight and eloquence who taught me a great deal about how to think about individuals and society, not to mention how to weave general insights into more personal ones. I was fortunate in acquiring the Standard Edition of *The Complete Psychological Works of Sigmund Freud*, trans. James Strachey (1953; Hogarth Press, 1971) early in my career and have consulted it in writing this book.

For references to philosophers, I have relied on *Great Conversation: A Historical Introduction*, by Norman Melchert and David R. Morrow (Oxford, 2018). Mikhail Bakhtin's work figures in some of these chapters; I consulted *Towards a Philosophy of the Act*, ed. Vadim Liapunov and Michael Holquist, trans. Vadim Liapunov (University of Texas Press, 1993), and *The Dialogic Imagination: Four Essays*, trans. Caryl Emerson and Michael Holquist (University of Texas Press, 1982). I am also indebted to the work of psychoanalyst Adam Phillips, an eclectic thinker much influenced by Freud and by Jewish scholarship. His most recent book, *On Wanting to Change* (Picador, 2022), succinctly encapsulates his style and range of interests.

In graduate school and throughout my career, I've been a student of Henry James. Around the same time that I acquired my complete Freud, I also acquired a complete New York Edition of *The Novels and Tales of Henry James*, 26 vols. (1907; Charles Scribner's Sons, 1960), which I use for references to the prefaces as well as the novels. Jane Austen has also been a touchstone—I adapted two of her novels into contemporary novels of manners, the first of which, *Jane Austen in Boca* (St. Martin's Press, 2003), I cite in discussing how I learned to write dialogue. My references to Austen are from the Penguin edition of her novels.

Some of what I say in this book derives from work spent studying family systems theory. I became interested in this material during time spent as an extern at the Child Guidance Clinic in Philadelphia, where I watched families talk behind a one-way mirror—a fascinating (literal) window on family conversation. Family systems theory has its origins in the work of the anthropologist Gregory Bateson, who gathered a cross-disciplinary group of researchers to study schizophrenia in the 1960s. Though the etiology of schizophrenia has since been determined to be largely biochemical, Bateson's essays on a range of topics in his *Steps to an Ecology of Mind* (University of Chicago Press, 1972) continue to offer a valuable way of thinking about family dynamics and group dynamics in general. The book contains the famous essay "Towards a Theory of Schizophrenia" and the "Metalogues" I mention between Bateson and his young daughter. I also quote from that daughter's later memoir of her parents: Mary Catherine Bateson's *With a*

Daughter's Eye: Memoir of Margaret Mead and Gregory Bateson (Harper Perennial, 2001). Like Freud, Bateson has been important to me in learning to think across difference and come to terms with complexity. For more on Bateson and the relationship of the family to the novel, relevant to my discussion of Jane Austen and Henry James, see my *The Daughter's Dilemma: Family Process and the Nineteenth-Century Novel* (University of Michigan Press, 1993).

The linguistic focus, present in Bateson's work, was amplified by the French theorists who used the research of linguist Ferdinand de Saussure to forge ideas about the "play of the signifier" as it connects to desire. I have drawn on my admittedly sketchy understanding of Jacques Derrida's *Of Grammatology* and Jacques Lacan's *Ecrits*, mostly as deciphered through rather tedious conversation with friends. These theorists' work began pervading academia when I was in graduate school in the late 1970s, but really deluged the humanities in the 1980s. I recently perused François Cusset's *French Theory: How Foucault, Derrida, Deleuze, and Co. Transformed the Intellectual Life of the U.S.*, trans. Jeff Fort (University of Minnesota Press, 2008). The book is mostly about the misreading of French theory by Americans. I am not in a position to critique this thesis but can vouch for the fact that the dominance of this theory in American graduate schools was detrimental to conversation in the humanities during the eighties and nineties.

Some of my references are simply the result of conversation with erudite and insightful friends and colleagues whose citations from their favorite authors have been incorporated into my lexicon. Some of these people also suggested that I consult certain authors. I am grateful, for example, to cultural anthropologist Robert Morais for directing me to Marcel Mauss and gift giving ("Forms and Functions of Exchange in Archaic Society"

[1925], available online at https://archive.org/details
/giftformsfunctio00maus). Morais also suggested the compari-
son between conversation and jazz and pointed me to *Flow and
the Foundations of Positive Psychology: The Collected Works of Mihaly Csikszentmihalyi* (Springer, 2014). Various ideas and citations from philosophers have their origin in conversations with
my late, great friend, Fred Abbate, whose insights on everything
from Aristotle to Aquinas to film noir to the pleasures of a hotel
bar I miss every day.

References to conversation etiquette come from my knowledge of Dale Carnegie courses (people I know have taken them,
and background is also available online). I came across numerous references to the influence of J. P. Mahaffy's *Principles of the
Art of Conversation* (1887), available online through Project
Gutenberg (https://www.gutenberg.org/ebooks/65638), and
I was charmed, as I note, by Milton Wright's *The Art of Conversation* (McGraw-Hill, 1936). Also useful was Deborah Tannen's
That's Not What I Meant! (Ballantine, 1986), as well as her work
on male and female conversational styles: *You Just Don't Under-
stand: Women and Men in Conversation* (Ballantine, 1990) and
Gender and Discourse (Oxford University Press, 1996).

After I drafted the analysis of Louis Malle's *My Dinner with
André*, Mariella Rudi revisited the film in the *New York Times*:
"*My Dinner with André* at 40: Still Serving Hot Takes," Octo-
ber 11, 2021. I would direct readers interested in movie talk to
Maria DiBattista's *Fast-Talking Dames* (Yale University Press,
2003) and to my own discussion of the transition from silent to
sound movies in *Silent Film and the Triumph of the American
Myth* (Oxford University Press, 2001).

The idea that close presidential friendships can mar diplomacy is from Joshua Keating's "Should World Leaders Be
Friends?," *Foreign Policy*, January 19, 2009. For Ronald Reagan's

PR strategy that I think changed presidential behavior with the media ever after, see "The President and the Press," *New York Times Magazine*, October 14, 1984.

The references to Joyce and Proust's conversation comes from Craig Brown's *Hello Goodbye Hello: A Circle of 101 Remarkable Meetings* (Simon & Shuster, 2012).

I am an admirer of Michel de Montaigne, inspired by my mother's lifelong devotion to his essays, and have taken quotes from his *Complete Essays* (1580), trans. Charles Cotton, ed. W. Carew Hazlitt (London: Reeves and Turner, 1877). My citation from Moliere's *The Misanthrope* (1666) is from Richard Wilbur's translation (United Play Service, 1998), though I read it in its original language in my high school AP French class—taught by mother! I draw my examples from Francois de la Rochefoucault's *Maxims* (1665), trans. John Heard Jr. (Dover, 2006), and my thoughts about French binary thinking and Descartes from Sudhir Hazareesingh's *How the French Think: An Affectionate Portrait of an Intellectual People* (Basic Books, 2015). Also illuminating in its discussion of France's "great chain of salons" is Peter Watson's recent *The French Mind: 400 Years of Romance, Revolution and Renewal* (Simon & Schuster, 2022).

New York Times reporter Roger Cohen happened to write about "bof, c'est normal" just as I was writing that the phrase "c'est normal" was a typically French way of moving beyond a contradiction ("Wes Anderson's Dream of France, and the Paris I Remember," *New York Times*, October 28, 2021). I also refer to the French passage in Thomas Mann's *The Magic Mountain* (1924), trans. John Woods (Knopf, 1995), a novel devoted to talk.

The Sarkozy attack on *La Princesse de Clèves* was the subject of my *Yale Review* essay, "*La Princesse de Clèves* and Nicolas Sarkozy," 101, no. 4 (October 2013). As for Madame Verdurin's "little clan," I am fresh out of a pandemic reading of Proust's seven-book novel, *In Search of Lost Time*, 3 vols., trans. C. K. Scott Montcrieff and Terence Kilmartin (Vintage, 1982), an arduous task that I wouldn't recommend to the faint of heart (I admit to being enervated by some portions but loved the catty gatherings at Madame Verdurin's salon).

On Plato's Academy, I am indebted to my philosopher friend Marilyn Piety, with whom I have conversed about the character of Socrates. I recently reread *The Republic* alongside her undergraduates and profited from her teaching. I also looked at Ward Farnsworth's *The Socratic Method: A Practitioner's Handbook* (Godine, 2021), and, though I critique the method to some extent, I agree with him that "Socrates didn't question people in order to teach us how to question people. He did it to teach us how to think." References to Cicero come from his *Treatises on Friendship and Old Age*, trans. Evelyn S. Shuckburgh (Good Press, 2019).

My knowledge of the British Romantic poets comes from having read the whole crew in graduate school and taught them sporadically to undergraduates. I would recommend Adam Sisman's *The Friendship: Wordsworth and Coleridge and Their Collaboration* (Viking, 2007) and Jack Stillinger's *Romantic Complexity: Keats, Coleridge, and Wordsworth* (University of Illinois Press, 2008). I also refer to the famous "Preface" (1798) by Wordsworth to his and Coleridge's first collection of poems, *Lyrical Ballads* (Penguin, 2007). Also see Coleridge's *Biographia Literaria* (1817; Thrift Books-Atlanta, 2009), for discussion of the *Lyrical Ballads* and its preface. As I note, Coleridge's style of brilliant, if relentless, monologuizing can be glimpsed in *Table Talk and the Omniana of Samuel Taylor Coleridge* (1835; Oxford University Press, 1917). I make use of material from Penelope Hughes-Hallet's *The Immortal Dinner: A Famous Evening of*

Genius and Laughter in Literary London, 1817 (New Amsterdam Books, 2000) with its evocative snapshot of Wordsworth, already venerable in 1817 when he was only forty-seven. As a contrast to Hughes-Hallet's depiction of Haydon's vanity dinner, I would point readers to Daisy Hay's *Dinner with Joseph Johnson: Books and Friendship in a Revolutionary Age* (Princeton University Press, 2022). She describes the "three o'clock dinners" held by bookseller Joseph Johnson in the 1790s for such eventual luminaries as the young Wordsworth, the feminist intellectual Mary Wollstonecraft, novelists Maria Edgeworth and Charlotte Smith, scientist Joseph Priestley, and painter Henry Fuseli. Joseph Johnson, it seems, was an exceptionally gracious and self-effacing host, and his gatherings forwarded the best kind of conversation and inspired great quantities of creative work.

On Shelley's Circle, I would recommend another work by Daisy Hay: *The Young Romantics: The Tangled Lives of English Poetry's Greatest Generation* (Farrar, Strauss and Giroux, 2010). *Frankenstein; or, The Modern Prometheus* (1831; Simon and Brown, 2012) contains an Author's Introduction where Mary Shelley recounts what occurred that inspired the writing of that novel. Also see my essay "Shell' Game: Mary Shelley's Poetic Journey" in *The Smart Set*, April 24, 2012 (https://www.thesmartset.com/article04241201/), in which I come down hard on Shelley's group based on my response to the exhibit "Shelley's Ghost" at the New York Public Library in 2012.

Many of the references to classical and canonical authors come from my trusty edition of the *Harvard Classics*, 52 vols., ed. Charles W. Eliot (1916; P. F. Collier & Sons, 1965), inherited from my husband's aunt and the basis for my essay in the *Wall Street Journal*, "A Year of 15-Minute Doses from the Harvard Classics," December 26, 2014. For a more comprehensive apologia for the Western literary tradition, see Roosevelt Mantas,

Rescuing Socrates: How the Great Books Changed My Life and Why They Matter for a New Generation (Princeton University Press, 2021).

Stephen Miller's *Conversation: A History of a Declining Art* (Yale University Press, 2006) is particularly strong on conversation in the eighteenth century, along with Leo Damrosch's *The Club: Johnson, Boswell, and the Friends Who Shaped an Age* (Yale University Press, 2019). Best of all is the original source, James Boswell's eccentric biography *The Life of Johnson* (1791; Oxford University Press, 1980), which I wrote about in "The Talking Life: *Boswell* and *Johnson*," *Boulevard* 17 (Fall 2001): 115–26 (some of the back-and-forth between Boswell and Johnson quoted in this book is also in the *Boulevard* essay).

On conversation as it influenced the founding of the American republic, see Akhil Reed Amar's *The Words That Made Us: America's Constitutional Conversation, 1760–1840* (Basic Books, 2021). For a general theory of conversation and opinion as it affects the public sphere, see Jürgen Habermas's *The Structural Transformation of the Public Sphere: An Inquiry into a Category of Bourgeois Society*, trans. Thomas Burger (1962; Polity, 1989).

I reference Virginia Woolf's *A Room of One's Own* (1929; Harcourt Brace, 1981), which has been important to me throughout my life; the two meals at "Oxbridge" continue to generate interesting responses whenever I discuss them with students. On the Bloomsbury Group, see *Virginia Woolf: Interviews and Recollections*, ed. J. H. Stape (University of Iowa Press, 1995) and *The Bloomsbury Group: A Collection of Memoirs and Commentary*, rev. ed., ed. S. P. Rosenbaum (University of Toronto Press, 1995).

For my discussion of the Paris expatriates, I drew on Hemingway's *A Moveable Feast*, the Restored Edition (1964), ed. Sean Hemingway (Scribner's, 2009), and on James Mellow's *Charmed Circle: Gertrude Stein and Company* (Henry Holt, 2003).

On the Algonquin Circle, I consulted Malcolm Goldstein's *George S. Kaufman: His Life, His Theater* (Oxford University Press, 1979) and James R. Gaines, *Wit's End: Days and Nights of the Algonquin Round Table* (Harcourt Brace, 1977).

On the *Partisan Review* Crowd, useful were Alexander Bloom's *Prodigal Sons: The New York Intellectuals and Their World* (Oxford University Press, 1986); William Barrett's *The Truants: Adventures among the Intellectuals* (Doubleday, 1982); Norman Podhoretz's *Making It* (1967; Harper Colophon, 1980); and Irving Howe's *Margin of Hope: An Intellectual Autobiography* (Harvest Books, 1984). I wrote about Podhoretz's book *Making It* in an essay in *TheSmartSet.com*, "Always a Critic," July 7, 2017 (https://www.thesmartset.com/always-a-critic/).

My understanding of the conversational vibrancy and depth that can arise among the members of Alcoholics Anonymous comes from a former student who is a member and group leader. I would also recommend Bateson's brilliant essay "The Cybernetics of Self: A Theory of Alcoholism" in his *Steps to an Ecology of Mind*.

I used the phrase "sublime conversation" in my 2014 Convocation Speech to the Drexel University community: https://drexel.edu/~/media/Files/now/pdfs/Paula%20Cohen%202014%20Convocation%20Speech.ashx?la=en.

References to the Harlem Renaissance come from the *Norton Anthology of African American Literature*, 3rd ed., ed. Henry Louis Gates Jr. and Valerie A. Smith (Norton, 2014), which contains excerpts from Langston Hughes's "The Big Sea" and Wallace Thurman's "Infants of the Spring." See Sandra E. Garcia, "The Rooms Where It Happened," *T: New York Times Magazine*, October 15, 2021, on the Harlem YMCA as a meeting place for the Harlem Renaissance. References to the Civil Rights Movement and the conversation with Elijah Muhammad are from

James Baldwin's *The Fire Next Time* (Vintage, 1992). The account of Leonard Bernstein's party for the Black Panthers comes from the article "Radical Chic: That Party at Lenny's" by Tom Wolfe in *New York Magazine*, June 8, 1970. I also reference Richard Wright's essay about time spent in the Communist Party, "I Tried to Be a Communist," published in two parts in the August and September 1944 issues of *The Atlantic*.

For more on gentlemen's clubs, see Anthony LeJeune's *The Gentlemen's Clubs of London*, photos by Malcolm Lewis (Mayflower Books, 1979), and on the feminization of culture, see Ann Douglas's book *The Feminization of American Culture* (Macmillan, 1998), whose outline holds for the English as well as the American fin de siècle. On separate spheres ideology, see Nina Auerbach, *Communities of Women* (Harvard University Press, 1978); Linda K. Kerber, "Separate Spheres, Female Worlds, Woman's Place: The Rhetoric of Women's History," *Journal of American History* 75, no. 1 (June 1988): 9–39; and Thorstein Veblen's *Theory of the Leisure Class* (1899). The idea has been central to much of my own work on the nineteenth-century novel. The repercussions of the shift from novel to film, and from words to moving images, is the thesis of my book *Silent Film and the Triumph of the American Myth*. Patricia Meyer Spacks's charming work of cultural criticism, *Gossip* (Knopf, 1985), notes that the term denotes a godparent, male or female, in Old English, and developed a negative connotation only when it became associated with women.

You can find some episodes of *The Civil Discourse* (formerly titled *The Drexel InterView*) on YouTube.

For material on comic duos, see Lawrence J. Epstein's *Mixed Nuts: America's Love Affair with Comedy Teams from Burns and Allen to Belushi and Aykroyd* (PublicAffairs, 2004).

I was reminded of the term "Harkness Table" by George Krall, former Drexel University trustee, when he visited the Pennoni Honors College at Bentley Hall, where I am dean, and saw our seminar rooms. Also see Andrew Delbanco's *College: What It Is and What It Should Be* (Princeton University Press, 2021) for an eloquent apologia for the value of the humanities. Delbanco laments the fact that education is stratified by class and has a view of the potential of higher education akin to my own. Testimonials to Donald Kagan's teaching style come from the tribute "Remembering Donald Kagan," *Yale Alumni Magazine*, November/December 2021. The position of the American Association of University Professors with regard to collegiality was recently clarified as it relates to civility and free speech in an online statement: https://www.aaup.org/issues/civility. Also important and inspiring is John Dewey's *Experience and Education* (1938), available online: https://www.schoolofeducators.com/wp-content/uploads/2011/12/EXPERIENCE-EDUCATION-JOHN-DEWEY.pdf.

Conversation theory was pioneered by Gordon Pask. See his *Conversation, Cognition, and Learning* (Elsevier, 1975). For discussion of how students of color feel in the college setting, see Beverly Daniel Tatum's *Why Do All the Black Kids Sit Together in the Cafeteria? And Other Conversations about Race* (Basic Books, 2017), and for the larger issue of how to talk about race, see Robert Livingston's *The Conversation: How Seeking and Speaking the Truth about Racism Can Radically Transform Individuals and Organizations* (Currency, 2021).

I often tell students who are afraid to participate in class that good conversation takes practice and point them to William James's essay "The Laws of Habit," in *Talks to Teachers and to Students on Some of Life's Ideals* (1888; Arc Manor, 2008); reprinted in more technical form in James's *Principles of Psychology*. This early work of intellectual self-help always inspires interesting conversation.

For more beyond my brief reference to affect theory and the affective turn in postmodern criticism, see *The Affect Theory Reader*, ed. Melissa Gregg and Gregory J. Seigworth (Duke University Press, 2010). I make reference to the value of touch as expressed by JoAnna Novak in the *New York Times*, "We're Longing for One Thing the Metaverse Can't Give Us," November 26, 2021. For more on Shakespeare and his dialogic nature that I believe increased over the course of his writing career, see my recent book *Of Human Kindness: What Shakespeare Teaches Us about Empathy* (Yale University Press, 2021). Part of the chapter "Shakespeare on Zoom" also appeared as an op-ed in the *Wall Street Journal*, "Reading Shakespeare in a Sea of Troubles," January 7, 2022.

The club that I mention that has been successful operating on Zoom during the pandemic is called the Franklin Inn Club, founded in 1902 in Philadelphia and occupying a historic building in Center City. It welcomes members of all ages, in person or on Zoom, and can be contacted at https://thefranklininn.com/history/.

Critical responses to Stephen Greenblatt's *The Swerve: How the World Became Modern* (Norton, 2011) appeared in the *Guardian*, *Los Angeles Times*, and *Washington Post*, among others. Thanks to Gresham Riley for discussing this book with me.

I refer to Leo Tolstoy's *War and Peace* (1865–69), trans. Richard Pevear and Larissa Volokhonsky (Vintage, 2008), and I am grateful to my students for helping me recognize the shift in the nature of Pierre Bezukhov's conversation.

Finally, I owe a special debt of gratitude to three individuals who were helpful to me in writing this book: Felicia Eth, my exceptionally broad-minded agent; Peter Dougherty, Princeton University Press editor at large, who encouraged me to write about conversation and gave insightful suggestions along the way; and Alan S. Penziner, my husband, whose sometimes brutal honesty in the tradition of Frank Capra ("burn the first two reels") has never failed to make my work better.

Index